A BROKEN MAN IN FLOWER

David Harsent has published thirteen volumes of poetry. *Legion* won the Forward Prize. *Night* was triple shortlisted in the UK and won the Griffin Poetry Prize. *Fire Songs* won the T.S. Eliot Prize. A new collection, *Loss*, appeared in 2020. *A Broken Man in Flower: versions of Yannis Ritsos* was published by Bloodaxe in 2023.

Harsent has collaborated with several composers, though most often with Harrison Birtwistle. Birtwistle/Harsent collaborations have been performed at major venues worldwide, including the Royal Opera House, the Salzburg Festival, the Concertgebouw and Carnegie Hall. He holds a number of fellowships, including Fellow of the Royal Society of Literature and Fellow of the Hellenic Authors Society. He is Professor Emeritus at the University of Roehampton.

Yannis Ritsos (1909-90) is generally considered to be – along with Cavafy, Seferis and Elytis – one of the most significant Greek poets of the last century. Because he supported the left, he suffered imprisonment or house arrest for many years, with his books banned repeatedly by successive dictators, from Metaxas to Papadoupolos. Twice nominated for the Nobel Prize, Ritsos won the Lenin Peace Prize, the former Soviet Union's highest literary honour, as well as numerous other international awards.

John Kittmer is a former British ambassador to Greece and chairs The Anglo-Hellenic League. He has degrees in classics and modern Greek, and wrote a prize-winning PhD thesis on Yannis Ritsos. He is preparing a previously unpublished manuscript by Ritsos for publication.

DAVID HARSENT

A Broken Man in Flower

versions of
YANNIS RITSOS

introduction by
JOHN KITTMER

BLOODAXE BOOKS

ISBN: 978 1 78037 649 3

First published 2023 by
Bloodaxe Books Ltd,
Eastburn,
South Park,
Hexham,
Northumberland NE46 1BS.

www.bloodaxebooks.com
For further information about Bloodaxe titles
please visit our website and join our mailing list
or write to the above address for a catalogue.

Supported using public funding by
**ARTS COUNCIL
ENGLAND**

Cover design: Neil Astley & Pamela Robertson-Pearce.

Digital reprint of the 2023 Bloodaxe Books edition.

To Patrick Davidson Roberts

ACKNOWLEDGEMENTS

The sequence *Homeland* was published as a pamphlet by Rack Press in 2021.

Other poems appeared in *Modern Poetry in Translation*, *One Hand Clapping*, *Poetry London* and *The Times Literary Supplement*.

A small number of these poems were first published in *In Secret* (Enitharmon Press, 2012) Thanks to Stephen Stuart-Smith for permission to reprint them here.

Special thanks are due to Yannis Ritsos's daughter Eri Ritsou for her kind permission as executor of his literary estate; to Irini Mavropoulou and her father Platon Maximos for permission to reproduce our cover photograph from his book of photographs of Yannis Ritsos's artwork; and to Dimitris Arvanitakis at Benaki Museum in Athens for providing the image.

CONTENTS

INTRODUCTION

I *Karlovasi on Samos, 2 April 1969*

Yannis Ritsos, under house arrest at Karlovasi on Samos, writes to his friend and publisher, Nana Kallianesi.

Nanaki, my sweet, kind, very dear friend, my unforgettable friend – the short message from you was a great pleasure, a reawakening of my soul, as were the books from you and those from Yorgos and Lena.[1] What to tell you? I've forgotten how to speak. Words fail me. So many, so very many have built up inside me that when I open my lips, they all burst out together, jamming my mouth and missing the target – they no longer know what to say, how to say it.

I want to impose some order: to speak slowly, carefully. But this is so at odds with the suffocation I feel within, with my innermost stress and anxiety, that I get the impression it's no longer I who am speaking, that it's just not me. My dear, I wish I could have recorded these dense, inner vibrations (mere noises really) automatically, without my writing-hand, my mind, my words getting in the way. The only thing that forms in my mouth is: choking, choking, choking, choking. And again: choking, choking. But at long last I must speak.

Let me tell you something of my inner 'life'. I'm not allowed to see anyone, I speak to no one. No one dares to come and see me. Every so often the authorities harass me. Three days after my arrival on Samos they checked up on me. They called me to gendarmerie headquarters. Then to army headquarters. Threats. Then they sent me a piece of paper so I could certify that they'd checked up on

---

1. 'Nanaki' is an affectionate diminutive of 'Nana'. Yorgos and Lena are the literary critic and editor G.P. Savvidis and his wife Lena.

me. Then they notified me by phone that I'm forbidden to move around. Then, again by phone, that I must seek permission for my every movement. The next day they come to my house to serve notice that if I'm going to travel, I must notify headquarters. Two days later, three or four of them come back to serve another notice saying that if I'm to move around I must ask for a special permit. Shortly after, a note comes from Athens: I must present myself there to the Aliens Department 'on account of my case'. Then, a second note from Athens: to present myself 'for examination', otherwise prosecution. At that time, I had blood in my urine again and told them I couldn't travel. Two medically certified letters needed, etc. etc. Then the commander from Vathy comes and summons me for examination: what contacts do I have with Theodorakis and am I – 'through third parties' – sending him my poems to set to music? Imagine: 'contacts'!

A week ago, they called my wife and asked her to sign a statement 'for her child's safety'. Naturally, she refused. Now we're waiting for new summonses. These are some of the external goings-on of my life here – to say nothing of their impact. You understand. Many times, when I'm walking on my own, at some lonely spot, on the road by the shore, a motorbike turns up with one or two of those gentlemen, and they loiter near me, conspicuously. Or in the early evening, they stand around at the corner of the road or outside the garden of the house, or they come to my wife's surgery to be examined as 'patients'.

Nanaki, I'm choking. Everything in our past seems like a mountain of fabrication: seeing each other face to face, talking, dreaming, publishing books; that quiet corner next to you, where I could sit for hours and talk, or say nothing at all – in that deep, comfortable feeling of human friendship. Really, was good fortune like that once ours? That sort of paradise? If so, we didn't give it the value it deserved. How is your husband? Little Olga? Melpo? Tsirkas? Frangias? Your two Nicks? Stamatis, my lawyer?[2] Savidis and Lena – whom I knew so briefly but liked so much and now I feel they're like friends – friends I'm missing a lot. Give them my thanks for the Cavafy books and for their concern. And how are Miranda, Tasos and little Fotis?[3] Nothing tastes so bitter as being without that child. There are moments when I feel as if a knife is being turned in my guts. To be unable to meet or correspond or phone each other! I do so want to make contact with our dear Chrysa and Nikiforos – to thank her for her deep understanding of my work, for her kind, discerning, humane introduction to the French publication.[4] And I wish I could have written to Eleni Beracha and to Memas Stavrou.[5] But how could I?

When the authorities first left me 'at liberty',[6] they gave me the letters that were being sent to me – or at least some of them. And it seems that at least some of my replies reached their destination. In November, but also in December and January, I got letters from France, England, America, Switzerland, Germany, Holland, Sweden, Czechoslovakia and also from Athens. I even got a few magazines and books. I was getting requests from every quarter for translation and publication of my books, or to introduce certain poems on the TV or the stage. It was quite something! I felt that there were still a few channels of communication with the world, that I wasn't wholly constricted, that poetry wasn't completely useless. I was

---

2. Among the friends and family mentioned are the novelists Melpo Axioti, Stratis Tsirkas and Andreas Frangias.

3. Ritsos had been friends with Tasos and Miranda Filiakos since the 1940s and lodged with them in Athens for many years. He was very close to their son Fotis.

4. Ritsos's friends the translator Chrysa Prokopaki and her husband Nikiforos Papandreou were living in exile in Paris, where Prokopaki would prove instrumental in enhancing Ritsos's reputation in France. In 1968, she published in French an introduction to Ritsos's work, with translations into French and a bibliography: Ch. Prokopaki, *Yannis Ritsos* (Paris: Seghers, 1968).

5. Two of Ritsos's friends from the literary and theatrical world.

6. He means when they first released him from prison into home detention, in October 1968.

able to think a little before sleep, to relax my face into a little smile, to find sleep possible, and to wake and work on poetry, and to kick against the depression of slavery.

And suddenly this too stopped. They wouldn't any longer give me letters, books, magazines. Nothing, nothing, nothing. Not even the invitations from the Hellenic American Union or the Goethe Institute that they always used to send me. People had written to me from Sweden about sending me 25 copies of a book of mine that was being published in Swedish as *Greklands folk*. The parcel never reached me. And in other letters people told me that they had written to me on this and that day of the month, three or four times and that I hadn't replied to them. But I hadn't received them! Every so often, they would give me something (clearly censored) and from this I would try to guess what people had been asking of me in the previous letters that I hadn't received. And now, nothing. They've blocked up even this small hole in the wall within which they've entombed me.

At New Year and on my name day[7] I got a few cards – including from Miranda, Tasos, Fotis. I was excited and replied to them. We sent a parcel with sweets on Tasos's name day, we sent cards on Miranda's birthday, we sent cards and a small gift on Fotis's name day, we sent cards again on 2 March for Fotis's birthday and 1000 drachs via Tzianoudakis. We got no response. We don't know if they got the parcel, the cards or our small gifts. We don't know if they replied and the authorities didn't give us their letters. We're worried in case something has happened to *them*, just because we wrote them letters. Please find out, Nana, and write to me about it, using the same means by which you will get this letter.

Every moment of the day, I'm consumed with anxiety for all of you – each of you separately and all of you together:

---

7. i.e. 7 January 1969.

for our ill-fated Greece. I don't know where this evil will end up. I'm striving to maintain my balance, to keep calm, to work, to sleep. I don't always manage. I dread my bed, I dread sleep. I sleep very badly. As soon as I lose the mind's control over my nervous system, terrible dreams are free to roam unchecked in my sleep. I drown in sweat. I shiver. I wake up. I close my eyes again. Worse nightmares haunt me. Day breaks. And it begins again: the suffocation of waiting for the next terrible thing.

When the weather's good, I go out alone for a walk. I look around. I try to see the sea, a tree, the mountain, a bird, a cloud, a house, another house, a door, a colour. Nothing. They don't exist. And even worse: 'They turn their backs on me, they avoid me – they fear incrimination.' And if some ordinary person does pass me close by, they lower their gaze, make out that they can't see me, to avoid saying 'hello' to me, or they completely avert their gaze in fear, and if they see that there isn't anyone following me, they greet me so hurriedly and guiltily and sorrowfully that I want to burst into tears or to apologise to them for bumping into me; that our country has been brought so low that people fear even to express love to one other and to say a mere 'good morning'.

Heavens above, where is our sense of Greekness, our *Romiosyne?* Occasionally, I think that this is all a bad hallucination, a crazy nightmare in a disturbed night's sleep. And one day we'll wake up and this bad dream will be over. I prefer it that way. I can't tolerate the idea that this suffocating slavery is *reality.* That's why I haven't even been able to write for several weeks. I fear that by writing I'll acquire full awareness of this shocking reality, that I will make this reality more *real.* Because poetry doesn't deal with half-measures: it goes all the way.

Once we used to say that poetry could be a way out, an exit from unpalatable reality. Now I know once more that poetry lives and moulds reality, making reality's reflections simpler and more vivid in the soul and in human consciousness. That's why I can't write. Even I need a little consolation and relaxation. And since at the moment I can't give anyone else a little consolation (consolation which I am myself in much need of), why write at all? In a half-finished poem that I was writing a couple of months ago, I was saying: 'What I need myself, I want to give to others.' Now I feel I can't do that. Later perhaps; yes, that may be so.

On Leros, even on Gyaros, it wasn't like this. Despite the deprivation and torments, and the pressures of being unbearably pushed around, you could find a few people to exchange a thought with, to say a few words to, to talk to about a book, about poetry, about painting, music, humanity. There were hundreds of 'fellow-sufferers' – a shared fate. You could sometimes pick out a tell-tale glance, a word, a gesture of human sympathy; you could sometimes manage a short 'conversation', a 'meeting'. Here, nothing. Only my poor wife, shattered by her exhausting work, by torments and by her worries for me, for the whole house. She props up all three of us. But sometimes a whole day passes without enough time for us to exchange two words. In rain and cold she's running around: to the villages, to the furthest outposts, even at night. Little Eri is at school all morning; in the afternoon, her homework. We see each other only at mealtime, lunch or evening. Falitsa is now so tired she can't keep her eyes open. My father-in-law, 87 years old, has had several strokes, causing him to lose all of his memory and his power of speech. He's still as kind as ever. Like me he stays all day shut up in his bedroom, on an armchair in front of the window, half-asleep and waiting for death.

Now and for the foreseeable future, this is my 'life'. My only props Falitsa and Eri – however little I see them. Even to read I have to push myself. I've half neglected my English, despite all the progress I made. I glance at the newspapers (all telling a similar story) in order to choke, in revulsion and nausea, at the madness, shamelessness and irresponsibility of certain people. Ha! and the hypocrisy of the foreigners: almost every one of those foreign 'democrats'! What should one write now? How to write? Why? And for whom?

On Leros I worked quite hard and may have done some good work. I wrote a big poem *Chrysothemis and the Eumenides*, a long series of *Testimonies*, another series *Stones*, yet another one – with 53 poems on the subject of ancient Greek myth and history, called *Repetitions*. And here, when I first arrived, I forced myself to work. I revised *Stones* and *Repetitions* three or four times. I wrote a lengthy poem, named *Ajax* – a tremendous failure. I rewrote it a second and a third time. Still a failure. I wrote a series of short poems with the title *Railings*. I still like quite a few of them, but I'm not in the mood to reread them. I worked several times on them, wrote them up in a good hand and put them to one side. Some notes that I've kept for a long poem have been neglected – I don't want to go through them; I'm afraid to look at them.

About my health – I don't know. I've left this to the last – so many worries weighing on my mind, you see. Really, I don't know. But I've been re-examined. For a whole month I had pain in my kidneys. I didn't even tell Falitsa, to avoid worrying her. Twice, on and off, I've had blood in my urine. And I had flu with a high temperature which knocked me out. Now I feel somewhat better. The idea of cancer won't go away, but has lost its intensity, in the face of other things that afflict my soul more. My only joy at this time has been the brave and honourable statement by Seferis.[8] He showed once again what a poet and what a man he is – these two things aren't ever separable. Good for him. I shake his hand and give him a brotherly kiss. This is the consolation that the true poet can give people. Our country can again be proud that it may be

---

8. A reference to Seferis's famous BBC broadcast of protest against the junta on 28 March 1969, just before the letter was written.

deficient in everything, but it's not deficient in its poets. And this isn't a small thing at all. Perhaps it may carry all else in its train.

My dear, dear Nana, write to me – you and all of you, when you can. Find a way. Send me some books. I need you more than ever. Perhaps a day will once more come when we can meet freely, look at each other freely, talk, publish books; when life, poetry and nature will regain their meaning and significance? My goodness, how I love you so, how I've missed you. I can't imagine that life in Athens is as terrible as on Samos. I've wanted to see you all so much, even if it were possible only for a brief moment: Chrysa, Miranda, Tasos and my little one Fotis, and Melpo, your husband, my lovely little Olga, your sister, Loula Christara, Frangias, Tsirkas, the two Nicks, Lena, Yiorgos, Leivaditis, Maria, our Athens – all of you, each and every one of you.

Don't forget me. You are unimaginably important to me. And you know, my dear Nana, what it means when such things are being said to you by *me*: me whom you characterised as wrapped-up in poetry. Endless kisses to all of you.

With all my boundless love,
    Yours, Yannis.

P.S. Nana, in the issue of the *TLS* you sent me, I see that I had already been sent an invitation to an international poetry festival in England.[9] Of course, this invitation – like so many others – didn't come. I've learned that in Zurich a book of mine with 49 poems from *Testimonies* (second series) has been published – a bilingual edition, in Greek

---

9. Ted Hughes had invited Ritsos to attend the Poetry International festival in London due to take place in the first quarter of 1970.

and in German – translated by Argyris Sfountouris.[10] Could you perhaps find a copy for me and send it to me? Perhaps through Vrettakos, who lives there.[11]

An anthology of seven Greek poets has also been published in German, with the title *Nights in the Security Service*.[12] I'm anthologised there. Translations by Vagelis Tsakiridis. The magazine *Der Spiegel* (8 January 1968) has an introduction to the anthology. Have you by any chance seen this book and the magazine? I haven't. I learnt about it when I was on Leros.

My book in Swedish was published by Wahlström & Widstrand, Banérgatan 37, Stockholm. Book title: *Greklands folk*. Could we perhaps get hold of a copy?

I'm vaguely aware of other books too that have been published: in Czech, Slovakian, Russian, Ukrainian, Hungarian, Spanish (from Cuba) – but I've seen none of them and don't even have any details about them. In these past two years, it's only Italy about which I'm completely in the dark, as to whether anything of mine has been translated there. At New Year I got a telegram of good wishes (only) from Pontani. Perhaps he knows.

I was notified when still on Gyaros that I'd been awarded the 'Lidice Medal' for my poem *The Last and the First Man from Lidice*.[13] I've heard nothing more. And, of course, I've never received any medal.

Now that they're completely blocking my post, I no longer know what's going on with the proposals made in different countries for translations of my work. Whatever I learn now has to come through you. I didn't even know that *Romiosyne* had been published in French. Nor did I have

---

10. J. Ritsos, *Zeugenaussagen* (Zurich: Propyläa 1968), pref. by E.N. Kazantzaki, intro. by M. Frisch, trans. by A.N. Sfountouris.

11. Ritsos's friend and compatriot, the left-wing poet Nikiforos Vrettakos (1912-1991) was living in exile in Zurich at this time.

12. *Neugriechische Gedichte (Anagnostakis, Gavalas, Katsaros, Patrikios, Ritsos, Vassilikos, Ziogas)* (Neuwied & Berlin: Luchterhand, 1967), trans. by V. Tsakiridis.

13. A long poem written at Prague in 1960.

any idea about my book in German (the one you sent me, my dear Nana). I was aware of the two other French books.

Thank you, my dear Nana, for your love, for your care, for your sweet kindness. Now that I've had this 'chat' with you,[14] I feel a weight off my shoulders. You have a good effect on me, you see. Even my voice has calmed down. And I've even shown some interest again in my poetry. Thank you.

> I kiss you on your beautiful Greek forehead,
> Please embrace all our friends for me,

> > With all my heart,
> > Yours,
> > Yannis.

10 April 1969. My sweet Nana, a little while ago, I heard your voice on the phone. You can understand my joy. I can't believe it. We shouldn't stop this means of contact, since, so far, they haven't forbidden it. I hadn't rung you for fear you wouldn't want to take my call – for fear that I would in some way expose you. Perhaps you too, from the same fear of exposing me, didn't give me a ring: a vicious circle. We mustn't, I think, fail to exploit the least "legal" wiggle-room that we're allowed. Tell our other friends. Let them send letters – simple ones, of course, and on literary subjects. Let's see if they give me any of them, now that they've cut all my correspondence with countries abroad. Kisses, kisses, kisses.

Translated by John Kittmer

---

14. He doesn't mean, at this point, that he and Nana have spoken; simply that writing to her in this intimate, open-hearted way has been a form of 'chat'. When he writes the second post-script, on 10 April, he and Nana have, finally, managed to speak by phone.

1

In Flower

He'd had enough. He wanted to scream.
There was no one to hear him. No one gave a damn.
His own voice frightened him.
He buried his voice in himself: an explosive silence.

If my body explodes, he thought, I'll gather the pieces in
    silence
and put myself back together.
If I happen to find a poppy (and perhaps a yellow lily)
I'll make them part of the pattern.

And that's how it is – a broken man in flower.

'A broken man in flower': an image that David Harsent
has skilfully enticed out of a poem in the collection *Gestures*,
written only a few months after Ritsos's highly personal
letter to Nana Kallianesi. As similarities between letter
and poem imply, the broken man of the poem was none
other than Ritsos himself: intolerably oppressed by the
dictatorship, exiled a long way from his beloved Athens,
unable to communicate or publish, wracked with psycho-
logical and physical torments, and isolated even within the
heart of his family. And yet, both the letter (particularly its
postscripts) and the poem show hints of the irrepressible
optimism and self-possession for which Ritsos was known
throughout his life, and which had already seen him safely
through personal, political and national vicissitudes and
traumas. Confined and under pressure, the poet chokes
and complains, he is close to silent explosion ('words built
up inside me'); but all of this can be offered as a form of
defiance and resistance: the broken man will flower again.

Ritsos's letter was written almost two years after a junta

of middle-ranking army officers ('the Colonels') had seized power in Athens and imposed a nationwide dictatorship. As a leading Communist writer and intellectual, Ritsos was one of the first to be rounded up, on 21 April 1967. After being held in Athens for ten days, he spent some 18 months in detention without trial, on island prison camps: first on Gyaros in the northern Cyclades (May and June 1967) and then at Partheni on Leros in the easterly Dodecanese (June 1967 to October 1968). He was more than acquainted with such conditions: from 1948 to 1952, he had been imprisoned in the notorious internment camps based on the islands of Makronisos and Ai-Strati, under the anti-Communist laws brought into force in the third and closing round of the Greek Civil War. As someone knowledgeable about camp life, he had already packed his bag when the dictators sent round their goons to bring him in. Now in his late fifties, he settled down once again into the well-known routines of political prisoners. He was too famous to become the victim of the Colonels' more monstrous brutalities. Tolerating the indignities and deprivations of prison life, he was able to write, expressing himself in small notebooks and on scraps of paper; he found companionship in friends, acquaintances, fellow Communists, admirers; and he even took to artistic improvisation: learning how to paint on stones, bones and the dried roots of dead reed plants (Platon Maximos's photograph of one such work is reproduced on the cover of this book).

An international outcry, led by writers such as Louis Aragon, would probably not have been cause enough for the junta to liberate him. But Ritsos was an ill man. He was always at risk from reappearance of the TB that had afflicted him on and off since his teenage years, and now he was suffering what turned out to be the early symptoms of bladder cancer. In August 1968, the junta finally, after two months of prevarication, sent him to Athens, for treatment at the hospital of Agios Savvas: the dictators no doubt saw it as politic to avoid the international opprobrium of causing the poet's death by negligence. And yet, astonishingly, they returned him to Leros scarcely a month later.

The Colonels had a general disregard for political prisoners' health and well-being, but Ritsos's persistent illness continued to represent a real threat to their image overseas. At the end of October 1968, the authorities released him from Leros and sent him to the island of Samos, in the north-eastern Aegean, placing him under house arrest at the family home in Karlovasi, on the north-west coast of the island. Perhaps they hoped that Ritsos's wife Falitsa, who was the local GP, would somehow care for him, despite the absence of oncological facilities on Samos.

House arrest was not generally intended to be a pleasant experience. It was one of a number of administrative techniques by which the dictatorship pressurised and harassed political opponents. Major democratic politicians, such as former prime ministers George Papandreou and Panayotis Kanellopoulos, recalcitrant newspaper owners such as Helen Vlachou, and many other opponents of the tyranny were subject to differing degrees of house arrest. Victims were usually locked up at home and unable to receive visitors. Outside, policemen kept watch day and night; in some cases (though not in Ritsos's case), security agents were posted inside, to follow and torment the victim even within the home. Ritsos's friend, the composer and former MP Mikis Theodorakis, received a double dose of punishment: he was exiled, along with his family, to the remote mountain village of Zatouna, in western Arcadia, where he had no family connexions, and there he was additionally put under absolute house arrest, unable to go out at all. The Colonels' cruelties were often brutal, sometimes petty and vindictive: Theodorakis's children were, for example, forced to sit apart from all the other children at the local school, to avoid 'contamination'.

Ritsos's letter to Kallianesi explains not only the particular form that his own house arrest took but also the psychological toll it exacted on him. The house where he was held is still today the Ritsos family home on Samos. It is a small property, five minutes' walk from the seashore. In the front part of the house was the surgery where Falitsa received patients and practised medicine. At the back, Ritsos had a small bedroom, where he kept some of his books and was able to write; the room looks out on the garden and the distant mountains. The house was home also to Ritsos's and Falitsa's teenage daughter Eri, who was at school on the island, and to Falitsa's ailing father. Ritsos was allowed to leave the house to walk locally, but he was followed wherever he went; locals were not allowed to speak to him or acknowledge him in any way. The junta intercepted and censored his letters, at times completely blocking receipt of correspondence. Very occasionally, the telephone rang and he was able to speak to friends, until the authorities caught up with what was happening and cut the line. The relative comfort of being at home was more than nullified by the constant isolation and surveillance; the absence of social, creative and comradely contacts weighed heavily.

Not only did he have to endure the psychological torments of confinement, Ritsos was also, as his letter makes clear, very ill, with incipient cancer of the urinary tract. At certain points, particularly in the first dark autumn of his house arrest in 1968, he appeared convinced that he had little time to live. Indeed, he decided, shortly after arriving on Samos, to protect his posthumous reputation by destroying hundreds of pages of unpublished manuscripts, some of them in draft, some of them in final form. He sent Falitsa to Athens to collect cases of papers from his flat and he selected works that he believed to be of lower quality. Among those he put to the flames were poems, novels and theatrical plays. This was the second time that the poet's archive suffered grievous loss; his pre-war archive in Athens had been tragically incinerated in 1944, when the friend to whom he had entrusted it panicked and torched it. Now the destruction was carried out at the poet's own request. Of these obliterated manuscripts only four theatrical plays were preserved elsewhere, to allow for subsequent publication; all else was gone for good.

Ritsos may have felt that only his detractors would be interested in his lesser unpublished material. And certainly, he had no imminent expectation that even his best work would be published again. On stealing power in April 1967, the Colonels had placed Ritsos's entire *oeuvre* on their index of proscribed books: his existing work could not be bought or sold, consulted in public libraries or even talked about. It was a reprise of the punishment meted out by the Metaxas Dictatorship in 1936. In addition, preventive censorship had been established, making it impossible for Ritsos to publish any new work. In protest at such restrictions almost all writers joined in an act of mutual solidarity, refusing to publish anything at all (the silence was eventually broken by Seferis's protest statement of March 1969, which Ritsos mentions admiringly in his letter to Kallianesi). The authorities took steps to ensure that Ritsos could not circumvent their controls. They were particularly exercised about the possibility of collaboration between Ritsos and Theodorakis. As the letter shows, Ritsos was subject to interrogation on Samos on this matter. He had, in fact, started to work with Theodorakis again in September 1968, when, newly returned to Leros, he received word, via a trusted intermediary, that Theodorakis, under house arrest in Zatouna, wanted him to supply him with resistance poems, to set to music. Ritsos answered the request immediately, by writing the bulk of *Homeland: Eighteen Bitter Songs*, but he had no means of getting them safely to his friend. In the interim, news of their admirable conspiracy seems to have leaked.

In October 1969, six months after Ritsos's letter to Kallianesi, the junta lifted its measures on preventive censorship, and in summer 1970, the index of proscribed books was abolished. The dictators were hoping, by these apparently liberalising gestures, to burnish their international credentials. Publishers still, however, ran the risk of legal action under the press law and other provisions of martial law. Sensing reawakened freedoms, writers started to test what might be possible under the new conditions. In January 1970, still under house arrest, Ritsos was allowed to go to Athens, to seek permission from the junta to travel to the Poetry International festival in London that year. (Ted Hughes, who founded the festival in 1967, had been one of the first to publish Ritsos's work in English, co-editing with Daniel Weissbort *Modern Poetry in Translation*'s 1968 issue devoted to Ritsos, Seferis, Elytis and other Greek poets.) As early as April 1969, Ritsos knew that there was an invitation to him to recite his poetry at the festival and he was eager to take it up. In Athens he was interviewed by no less a person than Stylianos Pattakos, the brutal and unsophisticated Minister of the Interior. Pattakos told Ritsos he could have his passport and go to London if he steered clear of criticising the junta. Ritsos rejected terms so obviously unacceptable to him and the meeting concluded on a bizarre note: something that Ritsos said made Pattakos realise for the first time, apparently, that Ritsos was a Communist. He was, nevertheless, allowed to stay in Athens for the duration of the poetry festival; as soon as it was over, in early April 1970, he was rearrested and sent back to house arrest on Samos.

Ritsos remained under these terms of confinement until November 1970. His health continued to deteriorate and the junta, once again faced with an unwelcome international outcry, definitively lifted his house arrest in that month, allowing him to return to Athens for emergency surgery, which was carried out in December 1970. The operation proved successful: Ritsos would live another two decades and in 1971, he was able to resume publication of his work: to flower once more.

2

For most people this combination of imprisonment, house arrest, ill health and poor treatment would surely have proved destructive of their powers of concentration, creativity and will. And yet throughout most of this period, from May 1967 until the final lifting of house arrest at the end of October 1970, Ritsos, who was in the habit of dating his poems according to their composition or revision, has left behind evidence of almost continuous work. In these years, there were only two periods – each of about six weeks – when he wrote little at all: in November and December of 1968, when he burned parts of his archive and prepared for death, and again in mid-February and March of 1969 when, as he explains to Kallianesi, he felt too suffocated to write. But at all other times, he kept up an astonishingly high rate of productivity.

In the months prior to the dictators' coup, Ritsos had been working in Athens on *Agamemnon*, *Persephone* and *Ismene*: three of the series of mythological monologues that would, in their collected publication as *The Fourth Dimension*, become identified as one of his most recognisable literary legacies. He seems not to have taken these works with him into internal exile and didn't return to them, to finish them off, until October 1970, as house arrest was being lifted. But he had also been working on a third series of the short, often mythological poems called *Testimonies*, two series of which he had already published before the rise of the dictatorship. The third series was concluded in Athens in early April 1967 but would not gain publication until 1989.

At first, Ritsos's work in exile continued in similar vein. On Gyaros in May 1967, he started the long mythological monologue *Chrysothemis*, which he continued on Leros and finally completed under house arrest on Samos in July 1970. At the same time on Gyaros, he also began a long quasi-theatrical piece *Female Messengers*, which he would finish off on Samos at the end of 1969. On Leros, he initiated the tortuous and, to the poet at least, unsatisfactory composition of another great monologue *Ajax*, which occupied him on and off from August 1967 until January 1969 on Samos. One might imagine that lengthy, intense compositions of this sort required conditions of stability

27

and permanence that were not features of life on either Gyaros or Leros. The greater part of Ritsos's work on these island prison camps was, therefore, given over to short poems, which form the basis of this volume of versions. From November 1967 till January 1968, he worked on the poems of the collection called *The Wall in the Mirror*; from March to October 1968, he wrote the second part of the largely mythological collection entitled *Repetitions* (the first part of which had been finished in 1965 but not yet published); and from May to October 1968, he wrote the collection *Stones*. Amid all of this activity, he got wind, in September 1968, of Theodorakis's request to him to write a resistance poem and drafted in response sixteen of the eighteen poems of *Homeland*.

Perhaps oddly, the conditions on Leros did in some ways suit Ritsos. He was able to establish a pattern of composition and reading, the two often going closely together. Scholarly analysis has shown that Ritsos composed the mythological poetry of *Repetitions* systematically, using his Greek copy of Jean Richepin's *Nouvelle Mythologie illustrée* as a prose source for the poems, each of which he tended to produce on a single day. This was typical of the deliberate, almost 'industrial' way of working that Ritsos adopted under more normal conditions. These poems are 'repetitions' in the sense that Greek mythology or history is often being replayed, with a pointed or ironic gesture towards the times in which Ritsos was writing. Heroism is reimagined as pure violence (the returning Odysseus presents himself to Penelope as a 'greybeard dappled with gore') or as decay (the Argonauts' great ship has become a stage-set for vulgar re-enactments); religion and its values have been upturned (a Greek community decides to dishonour its dead, to forestall the depredations of an unknown, possibly imaginary enemy); the nation's leaders are seen to lack legitimacy and transparency, the polity is degraded ('swallows have come back to the senate house').

These themes are crystallised in the non-mythological

poems of *Stones* and *The Wall in the Mirror*, also written on Leros. For the large part, these poems lack clear temporal and geographical reference. They appear to unfold in the harsh conditions of the Greek landscape (dominated by mountains, stones, black shadows, aridity and thistles) or in prison conditions associated with island camps (the handsome men of 'A Painting' are held within barbed wire, with 'sun, shade, a distant view of the sea'). The subject is alienated: abandoned and disinvited; marking time ('time will go on as it must'). He appears the victim of an unjust and inexplicable power (in 'Knowledge' the man in the dock is convicted of an unspecified crime apparently because of his silence). In an environment where all news is 'no news' (press censorship has reduced all journalism to the banality and sameness of state-directed propaganda), silence may, however, be his only weapon. In 'Double' the subject feeds his inner self: 'the hidden one…too clever to speak'. Looking into mirrors is a frightening experience, since they project a sort of hyper-reality, an unpalatably clear truth (the woman in 'At Dusk' sees in the mirror that she is wearing the dead dog's chain). In this unsettling milieu, the subject fears death (particularly so in the clearly autobiographical 'Cancer') but also toys with it as a form of ostentatious performance (as in 'Shame', where the subject merely threatens to kill himself).

The eighteen short poems of *Homeland* mark a decisive shift in mood. Theodorakis had asked Ritsos to write him a 'poem of Resistance…something simple, austere', and Ritsos, who had just been returned to prison on Leros from cancer surgery in Athens, responded with a collection quite unlike any of the others he was writing at this time. Sixteen of the poems were written in a single day, 16 September 1968; the final two were completed on Samos in May 1970. The poems are strictly metrical: each consists of a single stanza with four lines patterned in the fifteen-syllable metre of traditional folk song. Ritsos here achieved (in an image drawn from *Stones*) the 'fist raised above the wall'; the poetry draws on Greek history and its cultural symbols to muster the Greek people to wrench their freedom out of the Colonels' grip, biding their time when necessary. There are references to ballads of the Byzantine borderlands; motifs of popular religion; legends of the klephts' resistance to the Ottomans; Ritsos's two great poems of Resistance to the Nazi Occupation. However sophisticated and sinuously poetic the means of expression, this is a galvanising collection that was designed to move and inspire; in Theodorakis's musical setting of 1972, it proved immediately and wildly popular.

The mood of *Homeland* proved short-lived. Once transferred to Samos under house arrest, Ritsos began what turned out to be an unusually barren period, in which his confidence, battered by fears of death and a sense of suffocation, deserted him. In November 1968, he wrote a single short poem destined for the collection *Railings* but didn't return to composition until January 1969; and by the middle of the following month, he had reached another impasse. It wasn't until May 1969, after he had managed to phone Kallianesi and got his letter to her, that he was productive again. The period of absolute despair thus proved remarkably short-lived; his work now regained flight. In May and June 1969, he finally completed *Railings* and wrote from scratch the third series of *Repetitions*. After the hot summer months were over, he engaged in a continuous process of composition of both short and long poems. The series of short poems included: *Gestures* (September 1969 to January 1970); *Corridor and Stairs* (February and March 1970); *Hints* (May to October 1970); and *Of Paper, 1* (October and November 1970). The longer poems included: the quasi-theatrical *The Annihilation of Milos* (September to November 1969); the mythological monologue *Helen* (May to August 1970); the completion of *Chrysothemis* (in July 1970); and the *sui generis* poem *The Net* (August to September 1970).

While it shares some of the themes of Ritsos's poems from Leros, the poetry of house arrest represents a further shift in Ritsos's approach. Here the subject is caught up in a surreally bewildering and terrifying landscape. He is menaced by mysterious events: who has planted the incriminating evidence in 'Midnight Knock'? Can the subject of 'The Summons' avoid the immediate and inexplicable call to appear? What is happening in 'Just This', when the candle goes out and a letter is pushed under the door? Everywhere, unknown and unnamed forces appear to act against the subject's interests, spreading fear, causing suffocating claustrophobia and inertia. Things seem consistently inverted and reversed: inside is outside; houses are built above graves are built above houses; the dead and living have exchanged places (in 'From Nowhere to Nowhere' the tourist buses are 'packed with the long-since dead'; the people in 'Out in the Open' are 'the standing-dead' and the 'dead who lie down wide awake'). A statue changes place with a cyclist and takes flight. Those who stare from within the house at the passing hearse are themselves statues.

Surrounded and oppressed by the inexplicable, the impossible and the pointless, the subject fears a loss of his own identity (in 'Masquerade' the subject is 'looking for his face among an audience of masks'). Meaning has leached out of life; experience has attenuated, bringing the subject to a state of catatonic paralysis (in 'Himself Alone' everything has been reduced to 'small movements sanctified by repetition'). Death hovers in traps, around every corner: both banal and terrifying. Occasional glimpses of optimism (e.g. in 'Aware', where he hears three young women laughing: 'That laughter is all he wants') cannot dispel the overall sense of nightmare and absurdity. In these conditions, poetry itself struggles to maintain its coherence and unity. On the one hand, the subject in 'Testament' is emboldened to assert the world-fashioning creativity of poetry: 'I write lines: I exist. I write the world: the world exists'. On the other hand, the poet writes in 'Badge of Honour' with a 'broken stone in my mouth'; in 'Broken', the poet concludes that poetry is 'a write-off'. Ritsos's voice in these poems is fractured, divided within itself, ensnared in a theatre of the absurd, which can – through fittingly surreal poetic techniques – be performed and enacted but not parsed.

After the summer of 1970, Ritsos's books were no longer banned and, along with many other writers, he began, tentatively at first, to test the limits of what the liberalisation of the publishing rules might allow. His long and brilliant work *The Annihilation of Milos* was published in the provocative and instantly famous literary collection entitled *New Texts*, brought out by Kallianesi's publishing house Kedros in 1971. The following year, Kallianesi and Kedros recommenced publishing Ritsos's work in earnest: the Greek editions of *Stones, Repetitions, Railings; Helen; Gestures;* and *The Fourth Dimension* now appeared for the first time. The long silencing in Greece of the Greek Left's most famous poetic voice was over; the nightmare successfully survived. The poetry Ritsos would publish in the years ahead would set the seal on the junta's reputation for malign and deadly absurdity, proving, incidentally, hugely influential on a new generation of Greek writers.

3

In April 1969, Ritsos's letter to Kallianesi shows that he was now excited about the volume of international interest in translating his work. He had every right to be enthusiastic. Until his incarceration at the hands of the junta, the translation of his poetry into world languages had been patchy at best. Because of long-term advocates like Louis Aragon, he had been reasonably well served in French. Otherwise, prior to April 1967, substantial translations existed only in languages of countries under Soviet control: Romanian, Czech, Russian, Slovak, Albanian, Hungarian, Ukrainian and Bulgarian. There had been notably little interest in him in the anglophone world: the Greek-American translator Rae Dalven had published extracts of two long lyrical works as early as 1949, and showed renewed interest in his shorter poems in the first part of the 1960s.[15] But the most recent collected volumes of modern Greek poets translated into English for prestigious English publishing houses had wholly ignored Ritsos, to the benefit of one or two evidently lesser poets.[16]

As his impatient words to Kallianesi indirectly testify, the international outcry at Ritsos's arrest and continued detention by the junta had boosted international interest in his work, including in the UK. In 1968, Ted Hughes and Daniel Weissbort published Paul Merchant's translations of some of Ritsos's short poems of the early 1960s in an issue of *Modern Poetry in Translation* that was devoted to Greek work.[17] The following year, translations from Ritsos's *Testimonies I* and *II* (1963-1966) and from *Notes in Time's Margin* (1941) appeared in *The Review* in versions by Alan Page.[18] It is this publication that caught the attention and the imagination of David Harsent at that time and set him on course for a lifetime's interest in Ritsos's work. Also in 1969, Dan Georgakas published in the US a full translation of *Romiosyne* and, together with Eleni Paidoussi, an eclectic and somewhat amateurish selection of excerpts of long and short poems.[19]

This new-found global enthusiasm for Ritsos in translation prompted the poet to think hard about what he wanted

---

15. In 1949, Dalven published excerpts from 'Song to My Sister' and 'Spring Symphony' in her *Modern Greek Poetry* (New York: Gaer, 1949); in the early sixties, she published nine short poems in *Odyssey Review* (June 1962) and eleven more in *Poetry* (February 1964).

16. Edmund Keeley and Philip Sherrard's *Six Poets of Modern Greece* (London: Thames & Hudson, 1960) includes Cavafy, Sikelianos, Seferis, Elytis, Gatsos and the now little read Dimitrios I. Antoniou, but not Ritsos. Their later anthology for Penguin, *Four Greek Poets* (Harmondsworth: Penguin, 1966) includes Gatsos, on top of Cavafy, Seferis and Elytis, but not Ritsos.

17. 'Yannis Ritsos', *MPT* 4 (1968).

18. 'Poems of Yannis Ritsos', *The Review* 21.3 (1969).

19. Y. Ritsos, *Romiossini: The Story of the Greeks* (Paradise, CA: DustBooks, 1969); Y. Ritsos, *Romiossini and Other Poems* (Madison WI: Quixote Press, 1969).

translating and how he wanted it translated. Ritsos himself was an experienced translator of international poetry into Greek. Fluent in French, he had translated and published French poetry in Greek, as well as poetry drawn from languages he did not know. In the case of unfamiliar tongues, he worked off already published French translations or cribs in Greek, collaborating with native speakers to help him resolve difficulties of interpretation and form. By 1967, he had translated and published poetry from French (Paul Éluard), English (Peter Bowman), Russian (Vladimir Mayakovsky, Aleksandr Blok, Ilya Ehrenburg), Turkish (Nâzım Hikmet), Hungarian (Attila József), Ukrainian (Taras Shevchenko) and Spanish (Nicolás Guillén), alongside a volume of selected Romanian poets and one of Czechoslovak poets. He thus approached the translation of his own work with certain expectations of a professional, methodological kind.

Ritsos cared greatly about how his poems were selected for translation. He was a prolific writer and had been publishing continuously (with gaps during periods of dictatorship and proscription) since the late 1920s. His work had undergone several shifts of style, theme and poetic direction. There was an inevitable unevenness in the overall quality of the work, and anthologising was not an easy task. (Ritsos himself did not, for example, think highly of all his most politically partisan poems.) A satisfactory selection of translations would require good overall knowledge of the evolution of the poet's oeuvre, together with some sort of organising principle. Ritsos himself was more than willing to help. During the period when his work was proscribed by the junta and he was unable to publish new work in Greece, he succeeded in smuggling out some of his most recent material for publication abroad. In 1969, he sent to his friend Chrysa Prokopaki in Paris selections from the three series called *Stones*, *Repetitions* and *Railings*. The French publisher Gallimard brought them out in a bilingual edition in 1971, with the Greek originals reproduced next to French translations; Louis Aragon contributed the preface.[20] In the same year, Nikos Stangos published, with Cape Goliard Press, a set of translations into English of *Stones, Repetitions* and *Gestures*.[21] Ritsos had supplied Stangos with the poems directly. In both these cases, publication abroad preceded eventual publication in Greece, once censorship was lifted.

In an unpublished letter to Kallianesi of 1 October 1969, Ritsos expressed his irritation at the poor selections of his work made by his recent Swedish and German translators. Given the interception of his mail by the junta and the gaps in communication that ensued, it was perhaps inevitable that bad choices would be made. Determined to avoid a repeat of this in the selections of his work translated for the Poetry International festival of 1970 in London, he sent Kallianesi, on 7 October 1969, a daunting, long list of over forty works (some of them whole series of poems) to form his contribution to the festival. Perhaps in recognition of the vaunting ambition of that blueprint, he also included a more modest, short list of seven core works. Either way, it was a sign that he wanted to control the reception of his work by foreign audiences.

Ritsos cared also about the techniques and methods employed for translating. In a so far unpublished series of letters written to his English translator Nikos Stangos between April 1971 and April 1974, Ritsos explained what he took to be the principles of poetic translation. Perhaps surprisingly for someone who was not generally familiar with the original languages of the poetry he had translated and was reliant on intermediary French translations or on Greek cribs, Ritsos believed that the translator should achieve the most careful fidelity to the original, paying heed to

---

20. Y. Ritsos, *Pierres, Répétitions, Barreaux*, trans. C. Prokopaki, A. Vitez, G. Pierrat (Paris: Gallimard, 1971).

21. Y. Ritsos, *Gestures and Other Poems 1968-1970*, trans. N. Stangos (London: Cape Goliard Press, 1971).

stanza form and length, rhyming systems and sound, and seeking always to find precise lexical equivalence, where available. He knew, of course, that this could not always be achieved, but he put great stress on the skill of the translator in finding the greatest possible convergence with the source text. In his analysis and criticisms of Stangos's draft translations, he pushed Stangos towards a more literal translation of his original poetry, sometimes to the clear detriment of the ensuing translation.

Ritsos would, therefore, have been puzzled by the 'versioning' techniques used by English translator-poets, from Alexander Pope to David Harsent. Such techniques aim not to produce the closest, most literal translation that is consonant with a degree of poetic sensitivity, but to reimagine the source poem holistically as a successfully habituated poem in the target language. In the hands of a translator who is both alert to and appreciative of the voice of the original poetry and is himself a truly great poet in the target language, this approach yields great riches. And so it is with this selection of poems versioned by David Harsent.

I myself first became aware of David Harsent's interest in Ritsos when in the *TLS* (28 September 2007) I read his version 'The Wax Museum' from *The Wall in the Mirror* (reproduced in this collection). That version elegantly and spryly captures a mischievous side of Ritsos's lifelong obsession with statues. In 2012, I bought and admiringly read a copy of *In Secret*, Harsent's first volume of Ritsos versions.[22] I was intrigued not only by his versioning technique and the great poetry that ensued, but also by his astute selection of poems. Harsent had, it seemed to me, noticed something about Ritsos's poetry that most of the academic literature had somehow ignored, namely his

---

22. David Harsent, *In Secret: Versions of Yannis Ritsos* (London: Enitharmon Press, 2012).

sense that under the surfaces and superficies of things and situations subsist profound depths and necessary mysteries. This persistent aspect of Ritsos's work is perhaps surprising in a supposedly Marxist writer. I would call it metaphysical and locate it in the ages old traditions of Greek thought.

When David Harsent, therefore, proposed to me that we collaborate to produce a volume of translations, selected from the short poems that Ritsos wrote after his forced transfers to Gyaros and Leros and subsequently under house arrest at Karlovasi, I said yes: yes, enthusiastically. Collaborating with Harsent in the creation of this present volume has been a stimulating, moving experience. We started work in the first Covid-19 lockdown of 2020, sensing in our own circumstances some similarities with the conditions under which Ritsos had worked from 1967 to 1970. Like Ritsos, we were isolated and substantially alienated from our usual social networks. Fearing sickness and acutely aware of our mortality, we experienced some of the psychological stresses that Ritsos had felt, in far greater degree, in detention on the island camps and under house arrest on Samos.

Harsent worked his way through extensive examples of all nine series of short poems written during Ritsos's long period of confinement on Leros and Samos. The poems versioned in this collection are drawn from eight of those nine: *The Wall in the Mirror*; *Repetitions*; *Stones*; *Homeland*; *Railings*; *Gestures*; *Corridor and Stairs*; and *Hints*. As explained above, the poetry of this period has its own thematic logic and concerns, tied closely to the conditions of isolation and alienation experienced by the poet under an absurd and reactionary, but menacing dictatorship. The principle of selection employed for this volume is, therefore, one that would easily have been endorsed by Ritsos himself.

In versioning these poems in English, Harsent worked off already published English translations and from literal cribs that I prepared specially for him. By e-mail, text and phone, we had a regular dialogue, which proved challenging, instructive and, on Harsent's part, profoundly creative. Harsent would send me drafts, seeking reactions and often posing precise linguistic and cultural questions that had crossed his mind and perhaps puzzled him. Knowing no Greek, he wanted to understand, as far as possible, the poet's range of possible meanings and to find a suitable home for them in English. Every so often, in return, I would lightly query what I took to be a small misunderstanding on his part of Ritsos's original text. Another luminous, arresting and invariably more faithful version would then promptly appear. I was constantly astonished by the richness and depth that Harsent could conjure in English out of my mere linguistic approximations of Ritsos's Greek, and by the sensitivity and accuracy with which he could reimagine Ritsos as a poet fully in possession and mastery of our own language. It was a lesson in Harsent's humility and attentiveness as a translator of Ritsos, his sensitivity to Ritsos's voice, and his rightly acknowledged genius as an English poet.

In the conditions of our national lockdown, David Harsent succeeded in finding a real point of convergence with Ritsos. These versions of Ritsos reveal in English the deep, imaginative resonance of Ritsos's experiences of oppression, ill health, isolation and alienation. There is an intensity of vision to much of Ritsos's writing at this time. He was menaced and cut off and felt that death was stalking him. More prosaically, he also had to cope with stupendous boredom; the thinness of his daily experiences is palpable in many of the poems. He grasps at a diminished reality, at contact that lies ever out of reach. Occasional bouts of optimism only add to the emotional charge of laying bare a human life so palpably and unjustifiably under remorseless, pitiless pressure. David Harsent's lifelong interest in Yannis Ritsos and his posthumous collaboration with *him* in this volume are a joining of writing-hands and of mutually complementary creative powers across place, time and language; a profound and respectful exercise which Ritsos would surely have acknowledged as a magnificent expression of '*piitiki syntrofikotita*': poetic comradeship.

JOHN KITTMER
Scarborough, May 2022

Timeline of Ritsos's life and key work

1 MAY 1909	Birth in Monemvasia.
AUG./NOV. 1921	Death from TB of his older brother and his mother. Starts secondary school in Gytheio.
1924	First publication.
1925	In Athens, to enrol for university. Instead works in a legal firm.
1926	Shows first symptoms of TB. Returns to Monemvasia.
1927–1931	In TB sanatoria in Athens and Crete.
1934	Joins the Communist Party of Greece. Publishes *Tractors*, his first collection of poetry.
1936	His poem *Epitafios* attracts public attention and is burned by the Metaxas dictatorship.
1938	Takes up work in the Greek theatre.
APRIL 1941	Nazi invasion of Greece.
SEPTEMBER 1941	The Left-wing Resistance group EAM is formed. Ritsos joins.
OCTOBER 1944	Nazis evacuate Greece. Allied powers return.
JANUARY 1945	Leaves Athens, along with other members of the left-wing Resistance movement.
1945–1947	Writes his great Resistance poems, *Romiosyne* and *The Lady of the Vineyards*.
1948–1952	Arrested under the anti-Communist law and exiled to internment camps on Lemnos, Makronisos and Ai-Strati.
1956	Publishes *Moonlight Sonata*, which wins the First State Prize for Poetry in 1957.
1956–1962	Travels intermittently to the countries of the Warsaw Pact.
1963	Publishes *Twelve Poems for Cavafy* as his contribution to the Cavafy Centenary.
1963–1966	Publishes *Testimonies I* and *II*.
21 APRIL 1967	Arrested by the junta.
MAY–JUNE 1967	In detention on Gyaros.
JUNE 1967–OCT 1968	Transferred and held in detention at Partheni on Leros.
AUGUST 1968	In hospital in Athens for cancer treatment.
OCT 1968–NOV 1970	Under house arrest at Karlovasi on Samos.

OCTOBER 1969	The junta lifts preventive censorship.
SUMMER 1970	The junta abolishes the index of prescribed authors / books.
DECEMBER 1970	In hospital in Athens for further cancer treatment.
1971	Publishes *The Annihilation of Milos* as his contribution to *New Texts*.
1972	Regular publication of Ritsos's poetry begins again. Publishes *The Fourth Dimension*. Maria Delivorria succeeds in delivering the manuscript of *Homeland: Eighteen Bitter Songs* to Theodorakis in exile in Paris. He sets it to music immediately. First full performance at the Royal Albert Hall, London (1973).
1977	In Moscow to collect the Lenin Prize.
1982–1986	Publishes the nine autobiographical novels that together make up the *Iconostasis of Anonymous Saints*.
11 NOVEMBER 1990	Dies in Athens (aged 81). Buried in the cemetery of his hometown Monemvasia.
1991	Posthumous publication of Ritsos's many unpublished works begins with *Late, Very Late into the Night*.

[JK]

A BROKEN MAN IN FLOWER

I

Partheni Prison Camp, Leros

The Treaty

The Thirty Years Peace broke down.
Now there are plots and betrayals.
Old friends pass each other in silence,
old enemies become new friends overnight.
One cabal comes into town under darkness,
under darkness another leaves.

Statues in the city squares are streaked with grime.
In the public gardens the statues are caked with birdshit.
The pepper trees that line the streets grow thick with dust.
Trucks no longer spray streets in the midday heat.
But swallows have come back to the senate house.

People gather at the market. They ask: *Who are they?*
Where did they come from? Was there an election? I don't
remember that. They run the country now? Who says so?

Then a bird flies out from the colonnade.
A swallow! they shout: one voice, one people as before.
Look: a swallow! Then they fall silent,
suddenly alone. In that moment they know
that only by being alone can they be free.

Penelope

Not that she was fooled by his disguise:
she'd have known him by his scars for sure,
by the way he cast his eye
over the dead and dying suitors.

What was there to say? Twenty years of waking dreams,
now here he stood in the fire's last light,
a greybeard dappled with gore. 'Welcome,' she said,
in a voice she barely knew, he barely recognised.

Her loom cast latticed shadows on the ceiling.
The grave-cloth she'd worked to destroy
hung on the frame like something flayed.
Shapes in the weave darkened to ash
and lifted off, black birds of night
low on the skyline and disappearing fast.

The Plough

Once a hung jury would always mean acquittal.
Justice for one was justice for all.
We think back, as we watch a rainstreaked sunset,
and wonder if it was ever really like that.

At the ceremony of the ploughing of the fields
the priest would stoop to trace a cut
left by the first ploughshare
at the foot of the Acropolis and chant:
'Never refuse a stranger fire and water.
Never send a lost traveller the wrong way.
Never leave the dead unburied.
Never slaughter the bull that pulls the plough.'

Empty words, then as now.
Fire, yes, to burn your neighbour's crop.
Water, yes, to flood his fields.
The bull is butchered and hangs in some thief's barn
the apotropaic red ribbon round its neck.

A dead hand is laid to the plough
that turns the earth in fields where nothing grows
but mallow and wild lilies.

Unmarked

The Spartans stole Orestes' bones from Tegea.
Those relics gave them victory, which is why
our enemies will come for the bones of our dead heroes.
Such loss would be the end of us: our homes, our fields, our future.

*

Those enemies: who are they, where will they come from? No one knows.
So tear down the monuments, the statues, what are they to the dead?
Put up a simple stone, flowers, some cryptic sign or, better still,
leave them unmarked. In times like these,
we might dig up the bones ourselves and throw them into the sea.

The Argo

Half-eaten by worm, planks stove-in, tholepins and rowlocks gone:
we brought it to Corinth on a night in spring,
a torchlit procession through woodland, some hauling,
some dancing, and offered that broken shell to Poseidon.

Things grow old and spoil...

The priests chanted. An owl flew out from the darkness of the temple.
The dancers jumped aboard and improvised a masque: some rowing,
some mock-fighting: as if blood and sweat, as if then... An old sailor
watched for a while, then spat and walked off into the woods to take a piss.

The Studio

White limestone, hammers, chisels: think of it, men stripped off
for a life-class, athletes, muscular, each posed
like the next, legs spread as if for balance, one arm raised.

A skinny dog goes among them to drink foul water from a bucket.
It is scarred by ticks and sores. The statues are naked, heroic, beautiful.
Don't laugh, don't laugh. This is sad beyond words.

A Painting

They are down by the barbed wire, on canvas chairs, on stools,
in tree-shade, in patches of sunlight, reading, playing backgammon,
sitting silently... They are so beautiful. If someone made a painting,
it would look like this: men, sun, shade, a distant view of the sea.

They don't ask questions: the answers are nothing new.

Just this side of the treeline a skinny kid, a towel
thrown over his shoulder, is collecting bottles made cloudy by the sun.

A Break in Routine

They came to the door and read names from a list.
If you heard your name you had to get ready fast:
a busted suitcase, a bundle you might carry
over your shoulder, perhaps; forget the rest.

With each new departure, the place seemed to shrink.
Finally, those who were left agreed to bunk
in a single room, which no one thought odd.

They found an old alarm clock
and placed it just here, in the hearth,
a little household god,
and made a rota for who would wind it and set it
to ring at six-fifteen, in time for their needle-bath.

Once, it went off at midnight, whereat they woke
and sluiced themselves under the moon, then sat
in a circle round the clock
to smoke the last of their cigarettes.

Naked

Summer's end. Spiders in the crop-baskets,
lizards between cracks in the wall. He turns his back
on the statues: they haven't invited him in. His hands
rest on bare knees: to no purpose. Fingernails,
tufts of hair, a ring (some kind of ring). Mysterious.
He keeps no secrets, so has none to tell.

Growing Old

Saturday, Sunday, Saturday again;
now Monday as well...

A quiet, colourless dusk.
Trees gone to darkness.

We're penniless.
At supper: plates, glasses,
a half-empty pitcher,
pitiful hands of the abandoned.

A spoon is lifted;
it goes to the wrong mouth.
Someone is eating: who?
Someone is silent: who?

At the open window
a small forgotten moon gags on its own spit.

Blocked

Something more, but what? He doesn't know.
Add it to something, but what? He doesn't know.
What is it? He doesn't know, but feels it. His. His own.
He takes a cigarette from the pack and lights up.

A storm is rising, trees
in the churchyard will fall, but the wind
won't trouble the clocks, time will go on as it must:
chime nine, ten, eleven, twelve...chime one...

They are bringing plates to the table.
The old woman crosses herself.
Spoon goes to mouth. Bread falls to the floor.

Newspeak

Anything (words, birds, anything) now corrupted to symbol or slogan
was lost to him as love is lost; and 'anything' was almost everything.
So he stopped speaking. Like the dumb, he used gestures, equivocal, bitter,
    comical.
These, too, in time, they took for symbols or slogans.

The Wax Museum

In that dim light the naked, painted dummies
delivered a soft erotic charge. Their bodies
were perfect, as if they'd come
from a single mould, but when he looked more closely
he seemed to see his face among their faces.

There were footsteps in the hallway. He stripped off
and took his place, stone-still, with all the others
as the visitors toured the room. A woman said,
'They made a botch of this one,' then she laughed.
His eyelashes rustled as he closed his eyes.

Endgame

Outsized earthenware jars: one for each of us.
We eat, sleep, shit, give birth in the jars.

We die in the jars.

We might re-read last year's paper.
The news is much the same.

We dwell on murder.
Murder. Murder. Murder.

Oh, to smash this jar, to smash all the jars.

Blowflies swarm round the rim.
There's a brassiere snagged on the wire, rose-red in the dying sun.

Hindsight

One gone away, one killed. As for the the rest, who knows
what to say of them? It was no one's fault.

Seasons turn; oleanders come into bloom; as the sun
moves, so a shadow walks round the tree. That jug of water,
left out daylong, simmered in the heat.

We could have walked it round the tree
walking in shadow as the shadow walked,
finding a rhythm for that, a soundless music, until
there was nothing left of us but the shadow-dance.

Knowledge

He grew distant, silent, sad, and strangely calm,
as though he held some overwhelming secret,
knowledge beyond knowledge, beyond imagining.

'What?' we asked. 'What is it?' He stayed silent. Strangely calm.
You're not worthy, he seemed to say. You never will be.
We were his friends but, yes, we turned him in.

He stood silent in the dock and strangely calm.
They questioned, cross-questioned. Not a word.

The judge was enraged. 'Quiet!' he bellowed;
his gavel hammered the bench, 'Don't listen to his silences!'

The verdict came in.
One by one, we turned our faces to the wall.

The Blue Jug

Clouds on the face of the mountain, stones on the ground,
birds in the air. He walks a little way, then turns back.

The valley's a bed of thistles. Just one house;
in the window, a blue jug. Who's to blame for all this?

The poem shrugs him off.
Words are defined by what they dare not say.

Cancer

Suddenly, everything left him – trees, the sea, ideas, poetry;
or was he the one who'd left? He could sometimes make them out
on the far side of the river: seen, not seen. Death lay in him,
even to the tips of his fingers, to his fingernails. Each night
he could hear that monstrous weight as it shifted and grew.
Even so, before bed and again when he woke, he would brush
his teeth with that old threadbare brush: white smile, last smile.

On the Edge

'No,' he says, 'I can't decipher this; it's lost to meaning.'

A wind rattles the grass. Old women come to the window
and shake out bedsheets. The sheets are black. The milkman
pisses on the doorstep. The cripple sharpens a knife.

Flags are lowered on the battleship anchored offshore.
Bass drums roll downhill. A man with a shaven head breaks out.
He is naked. Each night, all night, he beats a mad tattoo
on kitchen pans. Prison guards come after him. 'He's mad,'
they yell. 'Don't listen to his mad talk.' Their bayonets catch the sun.

Women lift their dresses to hide their eyes.

Blockade

A flat calm. A light off the sea staining low clouds.
'If you don't look back, there's nothing to forget,' he says,
'live for today.' But which today is that?

Messengers come at night. They sit on the stone steps.
They unfold napkins and spread them on their knees.
One bears a scar that runs from his temple to his chin.
He stood up, tightening his belt, and pointed out to sea.

They have nothing to tell us. They fold the napkins and leave.
We set our lamps on the ground and watch our shadows
climb the white wall. Our shadow-selves are clumsy, big, and boneless.

Words

Words are much like stones. You could build a house
in which everything is white: chairs, tables, beds,
as long as someone will want to live in it, will want to lie
in that white bed or will, at least, sometimes come to peer
through the railings when the windowpanes flood red
and the bells of evening are rung from hill to hill.

*

(The bells fall silent. A bell-rope slaps the wall.)

Content

At night, the sound of a key turning in the lock. Just that.
You think about the key, it's shape; you think about the lock,
that simple device; you think about how key and lock will mesh.

There was nothing to be said about virtue or reward. So what
brought that unknown key to an unknown door? Some innocence?

The old doorman starts his rounds,
going naked, a white towel draped over his head.

Midnight

The arcade was in darkness. She was dressed in black.
Her footsteps on the stairs were feather-light.
'Halt!' they shouted, 'Halt!' Her violin was hidden
beneath her smock. She gripped it between her knees
and turned to them, hands raised, and smiling, smiling.

The Message

He rang the doorbell. Nothing.
Indoors, their faces: dim in the mirror; no one moved.
The sound circled the house and came back to him.

That was enough. He went to the gate pausing to cut
a flower which he slipped into his shirt.
Good, he thought, they didn't open up; it went to plan.

He hadn't been invited, he had no message to give.
But the sound of the bell
was a gift to them, a gift to him.

Things Shift

On all sides, the sound of water: deep, unstoppable, like you.
Ah, perhaps you're free.
Things shift in water, change shape, and you grow restless.

Later, some women come, and a few old men, to fill pots and pans.
Water holds its shape.
The river runs silently now. Doors open and close.

One woman held back. Now dusk comes in and the garden floods
with moonlight. She is of water: lucent, translucent,
a flower in her hair. Things shift. Perhaps she's free.

Double

There are two of him, one inside the other.
How could you ever know

since the hidden one
is too clever to speak? But watch

closely as he eats
a late dinner by lamplight,

you'll see him lift the fork
to his mouth slowly,

steadily, as a mother does
when feeding her child.

Her greedy, growing child.

Something and Nothing

Some men are killed, other men just die.
Hands, teeth, hair (mirrors).
They grow old and die. There's nothing new in this.

The lamp-glass broke.
We glued newspaper over the cracks.

Risks you should have taken are lost to you.
A long, slow silence and now it's summer again:
trees come into leaf, cicadas sing. Painful memories...

Blue shadows on the moutains deepen at evening.
Men come down the mountain path, bringing
their shadows with them; they limp, their shadows
limp in step. It's mummery; they're not lame.

Some dogs just die, other dogs are killed.
The mountain-men throw dead dogs in the river, tied in burlap sacks.
The men are sad and angry. They fold the unused sacks,
scratch their balls, watch moonlight as it scampers on the water.

But tell me: no one was watching, so why
did they come down the mountain path as cripples, limping?

Stones

A wind blew in from nowhere. The shutters creaked.
The leaf-fall was suddenly airborne, then gone.

Stones were left; just stones.

When night falls on the mountain,
a black door slams and locks. The key is in the well.

This is all we have, he said, stones, just stones, these stones.

I'll cut faces into them, nameless, and cut
the image of myself, fist raised above the wall.

Watermelons

'Stay here', they said. But for how long, no one knew.
It might have been hours or days. It might have been weeks or months.
It might have been for the best.

Oleanders below, cypresses above. Stones above that.
Birds flew in: black shadows over stone.
'Just the same in my day', the old man said. 'I could see iron bars
up at the windows long before they were fitted; I can't see them now, can you?'

A shout! The guards arrived with a barrow-load of melons.
The old man said, 'There's nothing wrong with my eyes
except I can't see a thing: whitewashed walls, sun, sea, salt:
an empty space looking back at me: whiteout.'

No bed, no chair, so you sit on the floor, tiny spiders
in your hair, in the hang of your clothes, in your open mouth.

No News

It's shameful, he said. Shameful.
He closed his eyes. He closed his ears.

What do you hear? What do you see?
What do you want? What will you give?

Seven bullets... Eight bullets...

Murderers will be murdered
and so on and etcetera.

The flags are worn to tatters.
None left to fly at half-mast.

Newspapers in the river
drift past the upturned face
of the drowning man.

All of Us

We're always on the move – from rented room
to rented room – table – chair – a bed
that's seen better days, straw mattress stained
with cum and the blood of bedbugs. 'It's the same
for all of us,' he says, 'and there's comfort in that. Consider
this tree, looking inward at its own blossoming, reflected
in the glass of a door to a garden no one owns.'

Convalescence

These colours make me nauseous, he says.
Light sticks in my throat.
I can't eat. Water turns my stomach.

Ah, but the long-stemmed water-glass: clear,
clean, fragile, holds its sad arabesque.
My contract with the glass is not to break it.

Shame

He went to the roof, to the edge.
'I'm going to jump,' he yelled.
The whole world held its breath.
He spread his arms as a bird might spread its wings.

*

He came down with his back to the ladder
face-front as the world looked on.
Some laughed, some were angry. In the end
they all applauded, except for those two women
who looked away. The third had already left.

In Short

The dog had the bird by its wing. Blood fell to the stones.
The hunter lay in the grass, an entry-wound at his temple.
Anyone stopping there would have called him handsome.
The dog looked at him, soft-eyed. It held the bird.

At Dusk

She went out to the garden. Someone had switched off the sunset.
The well had been capped. A small mirror hung on a branch
of the mulberry tree, giving back the flagstones and the dead dog's chain.
When she looked she was there in the mirror, wearing that self-same chain.

The Corridor

Gunfire. The women jumped up, tore chunks of bread from the loaf
and ran to their quarters. A white napkin fell to the floor.
The men continued to eat, untroubled. A woman came back,
picked up the napkin, folded it neatly, then left.
Her footsteps could be heard for an hour or more.

Ah! So the corridor must go all the way to —

II

Homeland

Eighteen Bitter Songs

Partheni Prison Camp / Samos

1: Baptism

Now words are re-born into bitterness, into agonies of song.
They have wings to fly. They have a dark music to make.

One word – *freedom* – is hidden from the rest. Its wings
are swords. Soon it will rise and hack into the wind.

2: Q&A

A cyclamen had taken root in the bare cliff-face. How
did this happen she wonders: strong stem, deep red petal.

The rock is blood-rich. I fed on it drop by drop and day by day;
it soaked me, bud and bloom. Now I turn my face to the sun.

3: In Time

We are waiting it out, so nights are longer and darker.
Our night-song seeded and grew; its roots go deep.

Some wait in exile, some lie each day in chains.
Their sighs are bitter...but the poplar comes into leaf.

4: The People

Fighting for bread, fighting for light and song: fighting
to bring bread and light and song to everyone.

No swords, no guns, but under their tongues the war-cry of the world.
Stones will shatter when they sing that song.

5: Memorial

Nine candles burn in the *koliva* – wheat-cake baked for the dead.
The old man on one side of the table, grandchildren on the other,

silent and still. Mothers tear at their hair and weep in silence.
From a high window Freedom watches; she sighs, unseen, unheard.

6: Dawn

Small dawn of springtime, graced by the sun, twice-graced…
How would it be to stand, eyes closed, in that pale light?

Sweet smoke from the incense burner, a cross
drawn in soot above the door that opens onto Greece.

7: 'Freedom'

The shadow of a bird catches his eye: he looks up
for the first time; a word comes to mind, unspoken.

That same word, or a curse: meaningless as the gun
hanging upside down from the pear tree as if in mourning.

8: Green

A girl sewing a shift for her dowry, a boy weaving baskets.
Myrtle and poppies, sheep on the hillside,

everything green and the sun shining through it.
The ram's bell, bells of goats grazing the coastline salt flats.

9: Theology

May Day. Birdsong in the poplar, a song of freedom
from men of the resistance: one tune, one tone.

The poplar leaves are candles to light the threshing floor
where Akritas met Death. An eagle riding a thermal calls our battle-hymn.

10: To Greece

A thin trickle of water from the rockface. Freedom-fighters
cup their hands to it. A bird's watchful eye, the shade

of the oleander, the mountain silence, all sanctify this.
The men dedicate their thirst to Greece laid waste.

11: The Song

Wind-blown cyclamen, like a hobbled bird now come
to the end of its tether. Sunlight strikes a glitter off its wings.

Its prison-dance catches your eye; the bird looks back at you.
You are fixed on it now. Soon you will sing the song it has forgotten.

12: Offshore Trees

They are strung out along the tideline harvesting salt – slim girls
bent like the offshore trees, bitter like salt. And here's a sail

white against blue, their only hope. As they work, they turn
their backs to the sea, to the sail. Now white is black—

13: Feast Day

A white country church: its bell rang all night
to mark the Feast of the Innocents.

Fierce morning sunlight. A volley of gunfire
from the narrow window to celebrate the day.

14: Epitaph

The freedom-fighter lies dead and face-up to the sun.
No need for burial, for tears or curses; there'll be no winding sheet,

no worm-tracks to score his cheek. That cross on his back
becomes wings. He flies up to join the eagles and the angels.

15: The Tides

Sunlight, abandoned beaches, wavebreak on the cliff-face.
Tides working day and night weaken the chains that bind us.

They might as well chain marble; they might as well try
to shackle the wind, or put a manacle on Greece.

16: The New House

Who will build the house? Who will dig the footings or hoist the roof-tree?
Where are the hands that will lift these unliftable stones?

Enough! Each day more hands, more men to bend their backs.
Each night the dead sign on and work till dawn.

17: One Thought

Here, now, there is only silence. Birds silent, church bells silent,
and this Greek, bitter, silent among his silent dead.

The whetstone is still. Our blades are dull.
But he sharpens his nails to talons and thinks of freedom.

18: No Tears For Romiosini

All that is Greece, all that is Greek, has a knife to its throat
and a noose round its neck: which is when

whatever it is that's Greek, whatever it is that's Greece,
reaches into the sky and arms itself with the sun.

III

Samos: house arrest

Abandoned

A woman died. They took her to the mortuary.
Canaries sang in the stairwells. All down the street
women gestured from windows. Then the garbage-man
right on time: kitchen-waste, boxes, parcel-string.

The dead forget they are forgotten. Their clothes
in wardrobes grow shabby where they hang.

The newlyweds posed for their photo. Suddenly it was midday.
Everything went dark. A door nailed shut. The blind man
looked through the keyhole, looked again, kept looking.

Poem

A group of houses set against sea and sky, perfect lines, perfect
colour-match, perfect harmony you might think, except
for the woman in this house, breaking a glass
against the kitchen counter (she takes the cutting-edge
to her wrist); the woman in this house, posing naked
before the mirror (on her shoulder a hydria); the woman
in this house, untangling from the mist-net nine dead birds
(a gift from the horseman). Women from the other houses
steal a look though this window, and this. They nudge each other: See?
Their men will leave at dawn to hunt the forest.

Ceremony

Mountains as always. Sky as always. As always,
five houses, two goats, a horse gone lame. A woman
dressed in black goes by; later, the postman calls; a bird flies through.

Plates are set in the kitchen. The old man comes downstairs.
His shadow falls on the table, the plates, twelve glasses.
They take the napkins – white linen, starched and spotless –
and tie them round their necks. They lower their spoons
to the empty plates then lift the empty spoons
to their empty mouths, slowly, carefully, until the meal is over.

As If Loukas

His face darkened by fear. They gave him back his watch.
His body bruised. They gave him back his belt.
His hair on end. They gave him back his comb.

Belt on first, or watch? Which pocket for the comb?
What to do for the best? No way to know.

He peered at his ID card. 'Loukas,' he said, then: 'Loukas.'
He kept his eyes lowered. He put his watch on, hurrying slowly.
He threaded his belt through the loops and pulled it tight.

He stepped into the hallway: a foul smell
from the ancient tile-and-trench urinals. In the street
a boy from the coffee shop was boxing empty bottles.
The voices of the guards echoed down the lightwell.

He said, 'Loukas...Loukas...' as if to a stranger, as if in a foreign tongue.
Lamps came on down the boulevard and in the museum garden.

Underwater

We watched, as before. A pine-tree lit by the sun, a green boat,
a rope, a gull's wing, soft light strewn on the water, then
a whisper, from the window, of consolation.

                                    The dead are at the threshold,
not sad, not angry. They hold torn nets, seaweed, crab shells that carry
painted images of a meek St Nicholas, a mournful blue Madonna.
All else left underwater. The divers see what's there but let it lie.

Fear

A hot night. Beneath the prison blankets, bodies contort:
angular marionettes. In dream, the blankets are beasts in a trap;
they have their claws at the sleepers' throats.

Someone
calls for water: everyone wakes. In the half-dark they can see
the stove, shut down for the night, and a black stain seeming to float
over hanging clothes.

They close their eyes; they bring their knees
to their chests; they pull the animal-blankets over their heads.

Did the stove have eyes? Will the black stain settle on them in the dark?

Substitution

In the garden, a statue half-hidden by lilies; beyond that,
railings, a road, a man on a bicycle. The statue watched.
We didn't see what passed between the statue and the cyclist.
What we did see was a naked statue on the bike making for the sea
and the cyclist on a plinth behind the lilies. It seems he forgot,
as he threw off his clothes, the amulet round his neck.
It made him more a statue than the statue.

Separate Ways

We never got news of Petros, nor of Alex.
They went their separate ways.
We never heard how things turned out for them.
We sat at the crossroads then, and here we sit.
We've rearranged things, put up some signs
though the wind brought them down in the end.
Truckers pass with oranges, apples, or grapes.
'Am I right for Argos?' they ask. 'Am I right for Sparta?'
We nod and wave them on as if to say
'We've lived here for years, you're on the right road, yes.'

Cigarette smoke pours from our nostrils. Perhaps they think
our heads are on fire and true knowledge a flame.
So, look, we're alive, we get by. We might force a smile
or pick our teeth like anyone. We know who we are, we know
when it's time for confession we'll have more than most to confess.

The View from Here

Almond trees, statues, snow-capped mountains, graves.

Gunshots from the olive grove.

A fine beauty, fine futility, as if it were sisters arguing
the futilities of beauty and life and death.

The hearse went by, heavy with almond blossom.

The statues stood at the windows staring out.

Just This

'Was that death?' he asked, as if just back from there.
The antique silver candlestick in his hand shed light
on the bed, the grimy sheets, snailtrack of sperm.

'And what...' The rest stuck in his throat.
A motorbike started up outside the window.
The candle went out. A letter came under the door.

Squaddies

Daybreak and still half-cut... They came out and squatted
to shit on the grass. They stared into the middle distance
and cursed their common enemy: 'Death – *fuck you!*'
The eastern sky grew light: a raw pink flush.
You wouldn't know whether they were pissing or tossing off,
but they certainly took their time.
                              When they got up,
they draped those broad battledress belts around their necks.
The heavy buckles clattered and clanged like sheep-bells.

Reversals

There are graves under the houses and houses
under the graves and linking the three
a broad stone staircase where the dead
go up and the living go down. They pass one another
wordlessly which might mean they don't know, or else
they're pretending not to know. You can smell
the orange grove on the hill; you can hear
children bowling barrel-hoops down the street.
Two women gossip as they fill their jug at the spring.
Their secrets cloud the water. Later they walk back
through an avenue of cypress trees
carrying the jug with care, as it might be a bastard child.

Kollyva

In the mirror, a headless torso.
On the chair a hand of stone, a young boy's hand.
A foot in a marble sandal
set as if to walk off through paper roses,
green asphodels, other useless things.

'These at least,' he says. 'At least we have these.
Not everything is lost.' Then, 'You know, in truth
nothing is lost,' he smiles through the lie,
'nothing at all.' 'Nothing,' the old woman says.
'Nothing is lost.' She sifts the wheat from the chaff
and boils it in a copper pot. 'Nothing,' she says.
'Nothing at all,' he says. Steam fills the kitchen.
They lean on each other and weep.

Aunt Laho brings in sugar on a tray,
puts it down, stands back,
then turns away licking her fingers.

Saturday 11 a.m.

Two women taking clothes down from the line.
Two men: one carries a suitcase, the other wears a black hat.
The dead pay no rent. (Eleni's phone has been cut off.)

The landlady stands in the doorway.

'Koulouria,' shouts the street vendor, 'warm koulouria.'
At the window, a young violinist. 'Koulouria,' he says, 'a tray
of big fat zeroes,' and thows his fiddle out onto the pavement.

The landlady rattles her keys.
The women go inside and shut the door.

Aware

Again, he says, 'No.' And then again, 'No.'

He turns his clothing inside out
he turns his glass upside down
he turns the water inside out.

He turns death inside out.

'You liar,' they say. They're angry now. 'You *liar*.'
He doesn't speak. A fly settles on his face.

Three young women (lovely, supple as willow)
sit out on a balcony, laughing. That laughter is all he wants.

Birdcall

Straw   string   stones   bones   bins   tins   dead men's shoes

A cold, clear sky.

A woman calls from the gully; her voice carries to another world.

Cars   cinema programmes   dead birds

Soon, we'll leave; night will come on; starlight…

Some have a voice: they speak. Some can hear: they listen.

But now, birdcall. The song is *Who are you? – Who am I?*

Why?

Things age, they wear out or grow useless:
bootleg tobacco, rooms boarded up, flags, statues,
that curtain once white now yellow. The useless dead.

The face in the mirror is scratched, or the mirror is scratched, or both.

The dress you wore that night is motheaten now.
The café on the corner shut down.
The balcony fell into the nettles.
The garden statue's cock has been knocked off.

Things age, they wear out.

So how to make sense of sorrow, of hatred,
of freedom, of freedom revoked?
What's the point of silver spoons, a savings account,
the dead woman's gold teeth, the sun, candlesticks, aspirin?

Of love? Of poetry?

Things wear out, or grow useless.

A hot July. They wrapped bread in a muslin cloth.
A small boat put out from the quay.
They floated a straw hat on the water,
filled it with newspapers and set them alight.

Connections

In the only room with a fireplace, a baby is crying.

A priest comes down the hillside.

(There are other hills beyond that.)

Snow   clouds   sunshine   windows.

A crow flies through. Its shadow strikes the ground.

Here...
Here...
Here...

Now not here.

In the not-here, a colour photograph of the local foortball team is lifted
    down the street on a cutting wind.

Wrong

He's taken an ice-pick to a block of ice.
He chips away. The cold numbs his hands.
He keeps at it. The wastage melts.

'I am sculpting the warmth,' he says, 'I'm sculpting
what's missing, what's most needed.'
He keeps at it. Water runs onto the floor:
you can hear it in the pipes behind the wall,
in the pipes under the floor, under the black
and white kitchen tiles, in the drainpipe out in the yard,
underground among the roots that drink it in.

The woman is ill. She calls from her bedroom.
He dries his hands on a towel and lights the lamp.
'It's done,' he shouts, 'it's done, I'll bring it in.'

Lamplight falls on the bed, the motheaten blankets.
Water runs in the gutters. They both hear that.

Out in the Open

Night after night, street after street, face after face.

Death-masks.

Somewhere a door opens, a window shuts.

(The dead woman's fridge was full.)

The blind line up at the underground station:
Let's buy a new car... *Let's buy a new apartment...*

(The shadow hid behind the curtain.)

A circus sets up in the square. Louspeakers roar
Roll up! Roll up!
Passers-by break into a run, then suddenly stop.

(They eat standing; they sleep standing; they fuck standing.)

He said, 'They are the standing-dead;
but the dead who lie down wide awake
burn eyeholes in the dark. We look through to see
faces, lights, cars, a turd, sperm, bones and bayonets.'

(He turned his face to the wall.)

We see an earthenware bowl, bread, a knife,
a woman with a fine big fish: catch of the day.

We see broken things. We see the staircase reversed.

The List

He is sewing buttons on his coat
using a man-sized needle and man-sized thread.
He talks to himself as he works:
'Have you had breakfast? How did you sleep?
Can you do simple things: speak or raise a hand?
Did you remember to go to the window. Did you
remember to look out? Someone knocked on the door.
Did you hear that? When you heard it, did you smile?'

One day it will be death. But freedom must come first.

Followed

These sunken eyes
follow you they are hidden
but they follow you
no point in disguise no point
in flight they follow you
they strip you naked
they register
your pointless movements
your pointless stillness
they follow you
they register
the broken bed
the toy sword
the seven masks
words poems glass
walls glass clothing glass
cigarettes broken glass

They called up the reservists
shift after shift old women
put to work
in the glass factory underground.

It goes on. Time goes on. It repeats.
The eyes are not glass.

Wait...wait...

...

No—nothing—

From Nowhere to Nowhere

Water on stone.
Water on stone in winter sun.
Cry of a bird.
Cry of a bird in an empty sky.

Water and bird-cry have the sound
of sorrows descending
on tourist buses packed with the long-since dead.

Circle

'Here's where I end and here's where I begin,' the voice
breathy and hoarse as always, as always the same image,
a circle and at its centre an empty bed, a table, a lamp,
someone peeling off black surgical gloves.

Plans

A bus on a country road hit the curve too fast.
Ambulances came and went, though most were killed.

A wheel rolled down the road. A local boy found it
and knocked up a wonky wheelbarrow. Now he sells
oranges in the town market; they glow like suns.

What came of all that: roadside wreckage, the dead,
a wheelbarrow piled with oranges? In a moment
we are gone. We make plans and promises
then, in a moment, forget them. And are forgotten.

Old Clothes

Then we put on those old clothes, patched
with scraps from the flag; in one pocket, shreds
of tobacco, in another, crumbs of black bread, a ticket
from the ferry to Salamis. A trace of gunpowder, perhaps.

The clothes are too big for us now, we're thinner and older,
thinking has tired us out. Sunlight flooded the windows
throwing patterns on the floor; an old bucket tipped
and trundled down the grand staircase. 'I'm not afraid of you' –
a child's voice up from the garden – 'but you're afraid of me.'

Memory's Thread

They came back when least expected: the view from the roof,
the well, a butterfly, corn-stalks, and birds going south:
a sudden rush of shadows. A horse shied as they flew past.

Men were loading a wagon with potatoes for local shops.
The waggoner went barefoot. Brute-handsome.
Town girls would lie with him in the thistle-beds at night.

Those vacancies seek us out from time to time,
memory's thread, it binds things long forgotten:
keys, a statue's broken hand, a fall of leaves, the wagoner's naked feet...
and you, who hoped to find meaning in this,
though your notebook was empty then, is empty now.

Himself Alone

He sits down. He wants to find peace. It's here.
That's a door, he's sure of it, and that's a window. Good.
Outside there are houses, a street, a garden. Good.
A leaf falls to the garden railings and holds for a moment. Good.

These things are lost to darkness, but still exist.
Get up. Light the lamp. Rinse the cup.
Change the water in the birdcage.
Small movements sanctified by repetition.

Frost

Pale light of November. Silence.
He put his head to the window: cold
at midday; but there's some strange source of warmth
to his back, a circular patch, as if thrown by the alarm-clock,
the whisky glass, the half-written poem. No – it comes
from that bowl of apples on the table, red one side,
yellow the other, Janus-faced like him: *excuses, excuses*.
Silence forms on the windowpane like frost.

Departures III

Things empty out.

Those bones you find on the beach in summer, bones
of something prehistoric, the marrow eaten-out, bone-white,
near-colourless – the shade rooms take in a downpour.

The doorknob under your hand, handle of a tea-cup, hand
over hand, impossible to know whether you hold them or they
hold you, whether they can be held, whether you can be held.

As you lift the cup to your lips you're left with just the handle,
white, near-weightless, a bone fragment, beautiful, but
it wants to be whole again: handle, cup, the tea you didn't drink.

Suspicion

Memories of that night: doors, walls, stairs, all in need of repair,
odd sounds: creak...*slither*...soft footsteps and whispers.

Wanting to enter, or wanting to leave – remember?
But the dead man's hand is on the latch.
Then the final bell and people going home. A dropped key
rings on the flagstones, a hand goes down to find it, yes...
Two shadows on the far wall pissing shadow-piss;
wagon-wheels across cobbles a couple of streets away.

Memories of silence, of three men moving from the colonnade
into the courtyard: smoke, cigarette-butts, paper napkins,
a clutter of overturned chairs. They are the uninvited.
They will have no say at tomorrow's conference.
One night, near-dead from exhaustion, they signed a paper.

Now they pick up the napkins, stuff them into their pockets,
and walk away, going carefully between the fallen chairs.

That Other Man

Three men at the window looking at the sea.
One spoke of the sea, another listened, the third
was fathoms deep. He floated up behind the glass,
clear in clear blue. In the wheelhouse of the sunken ship
he sounded the bell. Dead bell. A stream of bubbles broke softly.

Three men at the window. One asked, Did he drown?
The other nodded: Yes, he drowned. The drowned man
looked at them as a man might contemplate drowned men.

Numbers

Paper caught in a thornbush chatters and stutters.

A carpenter hammers a nail into a table.

Spiders cast webs on the underside of the vines.

A wall, once painted yellow, is peeling to grimy white.

A man tapes a list to a lamp-post: list of names.

A woman comes out of one house and goes into another.

(The numbers above the doors are meaningless.)

A caged canary sings in the dead man's window.

Absentee

He went from room to room. One room would be full
the next room empty. Between the two, nothing.
Then, further on, black and white chequerboard tiles.

Something struck the leg of the old iron bed.
Clang!
A brown overcoat under the sheets made the shape of the absent man.

In Reverse

Trees spread roots in mid-air.
The lovers go face to face between them.

One day, he'd gone down to the end of the garden
and thrown their keys in the well.

Roots in mid-air.

They look up.

On a high balcony, an old woman
is shitting into a flowerpot and eating an apple.

They agree to not notice that.

Soldier Dolls

Maps and lamps and engines and tanks on the uphill slope.
It's night. Everyone's running, shouting. *I can't tell friend from foe.*
Everything under a shroud of smoke. *Look up: there's the belfry.*
Yes, he says, *yes*, but can't see a thing. They take aim. He takes aim.

Women are left behind in the wreckage of houses. No beds.
Nowhere to lie down or sleep. They make dolls from the remnants
of army greatcoats peppered with bullet holes, or holes
burned by cigarettes when a soldier fell asleep or died in the snow.

They fill the dolls with bran and stain them with cochineal.
Children hang the dolls from a tree in the yard
and use them as slingshot targets. The game goes on till dark.

Waiting to Die

Dawn. His back to the wall. No blindfold. The firing squad
lining up on him. He seems lost in thought. 'I'm young and good-looking.
I wish I'd had time to shave. I like that pale pink blush on the horizon.
My balls have their right weight. Will they aim at my heart or my balls?

I am my own statue, here, naked, on a bright Greek summer morning,
set at the back of the crowd, behind the tourists with their baklava,
behind three old women, their black hats, their powder and paint.'

Almost

Nothing to be found in that dazzle; nothing you could dream up.
His belongings – brush, comb, ashtray – were no longer touchable,
nothing more than the simple objects they'd once been.

Silence had a hold on him, suffocating, warm, restful. Even so,
he could almost see, floating on the skim above his head,
a child's cardboard boat, orange peel, the drowned man's handkerchief.

Before She Sleeps

Eleven o'clock. She washes the dishes.
She tidies the place. Not a sound. She sits on the bed
and takes off her shoes, then stops.

Somehow, the day won't end. What's left to be done?
The house isn't right. The bed and the table aren't right.

She holds her stocking up to the light to find the tear
she felt earlier. Nothing. So is the tear in the wall
or perhaps in the mirror? Yes, it lets in the voice of the night.

The stocking throws a shadow, a net cast in cold water.
A yellow fish swims through it. Blind yellow fish.

Motionless

When she got up to answer the door,
her sewing basket spilled from her lap and spools
of thread went everywhere. A red one found its way
into the oil-lamp; a mauve one became trapped
in the mirror; a gold one... But no, she's never
worked with gold thread, so explain that away.

Another knock. She started to pick them up,
then stopped. Was there time for that? She stood
with hands at her sides, lost in the moment.
When she opened the door the caller had gone.

Poetry's like that. It's much like that with poetry.

Woodworm

The last of the grapes in an earthenware bowl.
The last service in the valley church, last candles snuffed,
last drift of incense over fields and hills.
The old woman is last to leave. She looks across the fields
to the hills, then to the clouds. In the silence she can hear
woodworm at work in the icon by the altar. She crosses herself,
her fingers sticky from the last of the season's grapes.

Omens

A storm at sea, sunlight lancing through it.
She watched a seabird cruising thermals.

That drift from raincloud to sunlight made her smile.

The bird came to her shoulder, a shiver of wings,
the weight of a pearl earring, no more.
Then she bowed her head and the bird was gone.

The governor's house on the hill was still ablaze.

White

Why the rain held off that night is anybody's guess.
Next morning, winter sun. A man shaving in a white
bathroom. An unseen hand wipes the mirror clean
with a white cloth. The razor is dull, it leaves
his cheeks patchy and raw. No one saw him go. No one
heard him. But that lingering smell of dime-store aftershave...

The Tree – The Hanged Man

– but leave him out: that vertical would break
the integrity of tree and sky,
the compositional balance, the way angles draw the eye.

A system of diagonals, perhaps…and find a way to paint
the density of the air, and give a hint
of a shadow's shadow moving free of the canvas, free of you –
birds in flight carrying his worn-out shoes above the city skyline.

That's it. Now a length of wire, a nail…
At the far end of the dining-room, in poor light, hang it there.

The Other House

Last night I found an obol in the ashtray.
Not mine: I've been through this house
many times, every room, every drawer,
every cupboard; I've looked behind pictures,
on the chimney-shelf, even under the jar
that no one else can lift. And not just here,
it's the same at the other place: I know
every corner, every inch of every room.

Next morning, I opened a window on a tree
that was never there before.
The branches were hung with mirrors,
silver bells, twists of thread, tiny sad
harlequins, small white birds stuffed
with flock and wired onto the branches.

The obol. The votive tree.

And as for that other house...

White Night

He pulls up in his sleep. He's had enough of that soft oblivion.
He summons himself: Stand here. He lifts the lamp; light falls
on the faces of sleeping men. They lie in wooden beds,
under rough blankets. He says, *I am the guard.*
Guard Insomniac. Guard of Innocent Sleep. Of innocent sleepers.
An old man opens one eye. *For God's sake kill that lamp.* He turns
his face to the wall, holding the light to his body like a thief.

Life in Phares

Bad luck has taken us to the edge: we read our future
in the shadows of wings, in the shape of leaves, how they fall.
We listen to whatever it was that can never be heard, we walk
backwards in our own footsteps. We go to the temple at night,
burn incense, fill the votive lamps with oil, leave our token
on the altar and whisper questions in the ear of God –
Where? What? How? – then go straight to the market
where the first word we hear will be the word of God.

It's never the answer we want, though perhaps we misheard.
So we go again: temple, lamps, token, the market till shutdown.
After dark we walk the streets, remaking what we heard
as metaphor, as anagram, but it never comes right.

This is our life in Phares: temple, market, word of God. Wrong word.

Midnight

Every night, on the stroke of twelve, the old woman
pushes back her hair with a strange, sharp gesture,
as if grabbing at the coattails of a burglar
half out of the window.
                    A moment later she wakes,
puts on her slippers and goes to the mirror.
She stares at herself. Her eyes are somewhere
behind the glass, looking back at spider-webs
and damp-stains. She can hear gold-leaf falling
in the courtyard, a snail on the padlocked door
of the storeroom; she can hear worms at work
in the flower pots and the old coffins.
                            The dead,
she tells herself, tread softly on softness.
Sometimes they slip into us – our bones
their coat-rack, our shoes their shoes.

Masquerade

He is looking for his face among an audience of masks –
black, red, yellow, blue, one gold with sequins sewn
round mouth and eyes, another with a flowing, showy beard.
He first wore that when he was ten. Now he's sixty. It still fits.

This one is white plaster, hollow-eyed, lacking a nose.
His death mask: he wore it often and it felt fine, although
he thought it might fuse with his face, become his face,
so it hangs on the wall, a clay pipe between its teeth, dark
glasses over empty sockets, a cold-eyed stare. *So make
another choice – the blue, perhaps, the black, the red, the gold.*

After Rain

After rain, birdsong is louder. After rain
mountains are higher and clouds half-fill the sky. After rain
everything is brighter: the walls of houses green
as never before, blue as never before.

After rain, the trees are clocks, old clocks
in need of repair, their workings laid open,
cogs and gears and springs. They run on, raindrops
ticking from branch to branch, erratic, out of sync,
bad-timing us into the future: *blind fate blind fate blind fate.*

Nausea

He talked a blue streak last night. This morning
words curdle in his gut. He's had his fill of words but can't throw up.
Workmen are painting the house across the street
a flat, crude white. In this thin air you can hear their every word.
One of them is dry-humping the chimney-stack. Thick, white gobbets of paint
splash down on black topsoil, on a mulch of fallen leaves.

Habit

Now colours, colours again, dead yellow, drab olive of dry vines,
sun-darkened roofs, clouds a dull white, white cold-cream
the old woman takes from the jar with the tips of her fingers,
almost without thinking. Her face is cross-hatched with wrinkles.
It's a lost cause and she knows it, just as she knows that poems
also age and die, that the mirror holds the image of her husband,
that he's still in love with her though loveless, that their wedding rings
are hidden in the grandfather clock, that the clock hasn't chimed in years.

Leaves

Words sometimes come as leaves come to the tree. The tree
is nurtured by sun and rain, by rich, dark soil, by fallen leaves.

Spiders spin webs on the leaves; they catch dust motes and dew.
Those patterns glitter with meaning. Under the leaf-cover

a girl is disembowelling a naked doll. A dewdrop falls
from a leaf into her hair. It chills her, limb to limb.

Quotidian

Things that shocked you once are commonplace.
You soon get used to it, he said. That's how it works.
The world grows pallid, colours fade, our eyes fade,
we look away from stained glass, strong lights,
we're more at home in hallways and cellars. It's no surprise
that rain starts up at dawn, that the town hall clock
strikes twelve at midday, that the hours between dawn and noon
stand out in the rain. Nor is it strange to find
this strange woman in the house, going from room to room,
hair uncombed, her stockings round her ankles.

Rain

It's raining. He goes out. He walks in the rain.
He comes back. He shakes the rain from his coat.
He hangs his coat in the hall. He goes upstairs.
He looks out of the window at the rain.
Some days it rains, some days not. It's meaningless.
There's a bunch of rusty keys on a bench in the basement.
For some reason, they come to mind. For some reason
it comes to mind that rain never shows in a mirror.

By the Window

The woman sits by the window, knitting.
The man kicks off his boots and stares at his feet:
how many miles, how many years, over bare earth, over ploughland?

Clouds are sunshot. In the valley, a church, the shadow of a church.
Newly-baked bread wrapped in cloth hangs from a tree.
A wind from the mountains finds the labyrinth under the stairs.

The woman sets aside her knitting. She kneels
and puts her hands into his boots.
Down on all fours she goes under the bed like a dog.

In Flower

He'd had enough. He wanted to scream.
There was no one to hear him. No one gave a damn.
His own voice frightened him.
He buried his voice in himself: an explosive silence.

If I explode, he thought, I'll gather the pieces in silence
and put myself back together.
If I happen to find a poppy (and perhaps a yellow lily)
I'll make them part of the pattern.

And that's how it is – a broken man in flower.

Three-storey House with Basement

Top floor: eight students, penniless.
First floor: five milliners, two dogs.
Ground floor: the landlord and his 'daughter'.
Basement: the lumber and the rats.

The rat-run goes to the roof by way of the chimney.
From up there, at night, you get a perfect view
of blackberry clouds, of gardens, the lights of cafés.

A train goes by; its after-shock
sings in the brickwork. One of the first-floor women
gets up, her mouth full of pins, and slams the shutter.

Call

The house is falling apart: walls, staircase, ceilings.
The furniture is falling apart: bed, table, sofa, grandfather clock.

Call a plumber, call an electrician, a painter, a carpenter, a builder.
I can't sleep. The taps drip through the night:

call

call

call

call

call

I think of their workstained hands: oil from the tools of their trade,
from whitewash, from drain-dirt, from the tomatoes they ate

by the light in the yard, or from pollen shed by the flower
they were given by the old house-maid – her secret.

Locked Off

First, travel was banned, then theatres and concerts. Ships
stayed at their moorings. The circus was silent, the big top empty.

Out of that silence came two pint-sized clowns, day-glo
baggy trousers, polka-dot shirts, each with a powdered face
and painted tear. They went through their stock of sight-gags
in the middle of the road. No one laughed. The clowns wept
through their powder, through their painted tears.
That night they were taken in chains to a certain building.

Next morning we woke early. The cages and wagons were gone,
the big top folded and gone, the square deserted. A false beard
lay under a tree. A boy put it on. He said, 'Santa. Santa Claus.'

Changes

He stands at the mirror to tie his tie. He's calm.
'The incomparable,' he says, 'the unalterable.'

There's a deck of cards scattered across the floor.
'Not death,' he says, 'that's the least of it.'

The café where we used to meet is closed now:
the Chit-Chat Café; that sign with its coffee-cup logo
(you could almost smell the coffee)
has gone; just peeling paint and broken grilles.

Chit-Chat...

There's nothing left to be said except
The incomparable, the unalterable, spoken softly
as if to comfort the dead.

Lies and Secrets

She runs through sunlight, hair tangling in the wind.
'I don't need you, I never did. I'm in love with the statues.'

She throws her arms around them, the *kouroi*, kissing them
on the mouth, the throat, the knee. Kissing their feet.

She falls to the ground covering her face with her hair,
laughing and crying. Beautiful…she is so beautiful.

One of the statues now wears her golden belt.

As Ever

In time, houses fall. A stove thrown out into the garden
falls, piece by rusty piece, just as the leaves of the quince tree fall.
Rain falls. Potholes in the road fill to the brim and spill.

Streetlights by the football-field come on.
The evening star comes up over the mountains.
The grocery store throws a blue glow from its doorway.
The bicycle throws a long shadow on wet tarmac.

That shadow, that weak light – you might make something of it.
(But poets are sometimes praised for their weakest work.)

Fakes

First he strips the face of flesh. Then he takes the eyes.
He peels the skin from the scalp. His line of work.

He arranges the flayed skulls on a shelf.
At night they sit under a green glow; by day

they are white and subdued, as if pain
had played no part. The dust in their eyesockets glitters.

'You and I,' he says, 'are fellows in this dark art.'
And that's right. He takes the heads right back to the bone,

but I build them up: hair and nose and ears stuck on with fishglue,
eyes of coloured glass, painted cheeks and lips touched in with care.

I place them at the window, face-front, a steady stare.
People going down to the town-beach smile and wave:

'Look, it's Petros!' 'There's Maria!' 'Yes, and Eleni, too!'
What I wanted for myself I wanted for everyone;

but Petros? Maria? Eleni? Who am I kidding?
What do I have to offer but coloured glass and fishglue?

Pointless

Drawn curtains, lamplight, cigarette smoke, a quiet night in.
Flowers in vases: white, a heavy fragrance, their shadows
cast on the walls, on the bed, on her naked body…that most of all.

Down in the basement, they are beating out metal
to make a shield. The hammer blows run through the house. Shards drop
from the mirror; paint flakes from the watchful face of that old hypocrite

The Girl Who Regained Her Sight

'For years my eyes were lost to me: black pebbles in black water.
But now, look: a cloud, a rose. Have I got that right? Tell me I have...

And this is a leaf. It's green. *Green.* I can see it and I can say it.
Can you hear me? Speech and sight, they call it freedom don't they?

Wait... The tray in the basement; in the basement
the boxes, the balls of string, the cages. I'd forgotten...'

Interrogation Centre

A hallway of doors. A smell of smoke. At the far end
five men in black, wearing identical masks, watched as he knocked
at each of the doors in turn. No answer. The men stayed put.
What next? It was getting dark. He made for the door to the street
but it slammed shut. Rain beat on the tin roof,
on the flagstones in the yard. He knew the wet street would hold
a reflection of the new barbershop, its plate glass window,
the blue leather chairs. He had just enough time to take a fix on that.

Locked

He tried the iron door. The iron door was locked.
He traced the wall to find the window. No window.
Water beneath the floor. Water – a running sewer.

He punched the wall and waited. Nothing.
Again. Again. His fist on the wall. No pain.

He felt in his pocket for matches.
A hand shoved his face to the wall.

Footsteps on the gangway. Guards went past:
left, right, left, right, radios blaring. It's night.

The piss-pail, unbreathable air, the iron hook, the wire...

Left-right left-right left-right. It's night. It's night. It's night.

Badge of Honour

Hammers at work: broken iron, broken stone, then unbroken silence.
Somewhere over there a hallway of doors, stairs, lights,
musicians from a foreign country, lamps in the garden-trees,
diplomats, distinguished guests, journalists, introductions,
much fawning and smiling. 'Tomorrow, yes, tomorrow, see you then.'

Dismissals, resignations. The unchanging changed.
They change clothes, change hats, change ranks and titles.
A rope tied off to a beam.
'Death,' he used to say, 'is rank or title. Death is a badge of honour.'

In the basement naked soldiers are making foreign music
with their bayonets on urns and cooking pots.
He is at his desk, holding a stone in his mouth.

I'm writing this with a broken stone in my mouth.

Midnight Knock

Come in – I've nothing to hide – come in – make your search –
no problem – I've nothing to hide – so, now – the bedroom –
the study – the dining room – and here's the attic – full of old stuff –
things wear out don't they? – wear out – so, now – a thimble –
that was my mother's – mother's oil lamp – mother's umbrella –
she loved me you know – a fake ID card – no – this jewellery –
not mine – no, no – this grimy towel – this theatre ticket – this shirt
with the holes and bloodstains – no, no, no – this photograph inscribed
to a stranger – well, yes, it's him – it's him all right – wearing
a woman's hat trimmed with flowers – who planted these in here? –

who planted these? –

who planted these in here? –

This

Each night a convoy of trucks goes through
carrying gas masks and drums of barbed wire.
At daybreak, down by the stone house,
the outriders kick-start their motorbikes.

A man in red appears on the roof. Ghost-pale.
He looks at the shuttered windows, at the hills beyond,
and lifts a skinny finger to count the nest-holes
in a dovecote from which the doves have long since flown.

The Green Armchair

This was the dead man's armchair, green velvet, the nap
on the arms worn to a shine.
When they moved his body the blowflies stayed with the chair.

Those winter mornings you couldn't tell day from daybreak.
The orange crop was heavy.
They dumped the wastage over the fences of storage yards.

In that thin dawn light, decorators came to the house.
The dead man's servant
gave them his master's neckties, blue, yellow, black.

They winked at him, took their brushes and paint and walked away.
Now the armchair is in the basement, a mousetrap
on the cushion where once the dead man sat.

Sleepless

Plaster dropped from the ceiling onto the bed at night.
There was nowhere to sleep. The mirror was broken.

The statue in the hall was grimed with soot:
untouchable – unfuckable – or you'd come away
stained black on your thighs and knees and hands and lips.

They cut the water off months before, then the power
then the telephone. The marble-topped table in the kitchen
was littered with cigarette butts and two large lettuces falling to rot.

Baptism of Blood

Then there was blood on the pavement, just a stain, but soon
the courtyard was ankle-deep. A chair went under;
the well filled up; nothing showed
but a meagre hank of rope between windlass and bucket.

The post office – the cathedral clock – washed red; red
roofs, red trees, red sun...
As the blood-tide swamped us we stood
shoulder to shoulder, innocent and beautiful as before.

The Summons

It was clear enough:
You are summoned to appear at once...
Nothing to say where or when.
No department, no judge, no reason.
He turned it over. Blank.

He read it again... *at once...*
He put it under his mattress, changed his mind,
put it under the junk in a cupboard, changed his mind,
mailed it between the floorboards,
closed the shutters, locked the door.

Later he changed his mind, went back, retrieved it.
He shot a quick glance at the mirror,
checked behind the curtain, went to the bathroom, tore it,
tore it again, threw the scraps in the lavatory bowl.

As he reached to flush it away
the first man grabbed his hand, the other two
took him by the shoulders.

...at once...at once...at once...

Renewal

Untended year on year, the garden came into bloom. Suddenly
there were flowers thick to the fence:
roses, carnations, sweet peas, a flood of colour.

Then that woman, beautiful as before, going through
with her watering can…and, as we watched,
the garden reached up, took her into its arms,

then lifted off: roses, carnations, sweet peas, the woman, the flowers.
Soon it was sky-high.
Drops from the watering can fell softly to our lips.

In Readiness

The house would fill with shadows if I let it.
I light the lamps, I light the chandeliers.
In every room, lanterns and candles and matches.
Either side of the stairs, tall candlesticks.

I strike the wall with my walking-stick.
I say 'walking-stick' out loud, then I say 'wall'.
If I name them I know what's what.

I have answers to unasked questions.
I have receipts and bills properly sorted and filed.

Now – and this matters most – I set a candle
at each corner of the bed (can you see?) and lay
a white ribbon nearby. A ribbon to bind my hands.

Report

Sometime later Yiorgos rode in on a bike. He was carrying
a guitar with broken strings. The cathedral clock backlit;
trash in the gutter; a cold wind in the trees; gunfire in the hills.

He said, 'We've brought the bodies down to the warehouse
but no songs, no flags, no tears, OK? I've made a list,
names and ages cross-referenced with their shoe-size. Hide it.
The three stonemasons were killed; that marble angel is still
headless, so if you have a spare… That's it.' He left the guitar.

Greece

Vangelis never came back. The house has been locked
and the shutters up for years. Dead vines, thorn-bushes, stones,
the garden patch laid waste. A broken jug.

There's a view of the sea if you look beyond the stable.
He sold the horse but that didn't save the day.
A bay gelding with white fetlocks, I remember...

A seagull shed a feather. An old woman sat in her doorway.
The feather fell at her feet. She said:
'Small moments such as that can seem a blessing.'

That man in the doorway opposite seemed lost in thought,
but he crossed himself and went to her and stooped
as if to kiss her hand, or lift the feather.

Hints

Explain this: breath of the infinite, the merest trace
of clarity, scent of the rose they set on a bench
near the wristwatch of the executed man.

*

That ancient coin in your pocket: had you forgotten?
Your finger traces the young god's nakedness.

*

The match ended, the stadium emptied out. The moon
fell into the net: a punctured ball. After a while,
the asylum emptied out. The inmates chose sides.
One wore a trickster's cap and bells. Women dreamed
the mad music of the bells and cried in their sleep.

*

The stowaway holed-up in the luggage van
among cases and trunks and bags. He felt safe,
the beat of the wheels, the thrum of wind.
But when the train pulled in to a station, surely
the silence would betray him. Porters would come
to offload. They'd see the buttons had been cut
from his uniform, see the blood from his wound
on the cases and trunks and bags.

*

Want to know what's truly important about art?
I'll tell you. It's everything you leave out, whether or not
you mean to, like that knife in the basket there, hidden
under the grapes. Under those purple grapes.

*

In the land of blind horses, they're pouring more void in the void.
Thistles, stones, wire, bones. Flies crowd a spillage of vinegar.
Everything's broken down but the ceiling-fan, *tik-tik*.
Three petty criminals, lying side by side and fast asleep.

*

Spring, cicadas, a plane tree, and the statue you ordered
laid out on the grass piece on piece. They broke it.
You might say it's sleeping. Perhaps. But we are awake.

*

A wrecked landscape, scoured and broken;
dry seas of the moon.

Land of pits and pitfalls. Of refusal; of refusal refused.
Blind lizards. Wingless birds.

They pegged the clothes of the executed
to the execution wall.

*

No gift of words all year. Even so, his lamp
burns all night
in case a poem should stumble in.

*

The moon sheds light, a slow release.
The stars let slip a soft wind.
A flower from the chaste-tree falls onto her breast.
She takes its scent... and, yes, the perfect choice.

*

His work-boots were on the chair,
he was in the far room, standing naked.
Nothing much to be said: boots, chair, the cheap
working-class pink. A still life, not a portrait.
But the smell of him lay on the air.

*

A man standing in darkness smiles a secret smile.
Is that because he can see in the dark? Maybe; or maybe
because he can see the dark.

*

The sunflowers almost hide the wall, the wall
hides the road completely. Beyond that you've got houses,
trees, hills, certain wrongdoings... In the heat of the day,
men from the lumber-yard go down to take a piss.
At night the dead come out to whitewash the wall.

Broken

What day is it? Monday? Saturday? Wednesday come round again?
Doors and windows. A certain colour
that might be violet or purple or blue. A cypress. A torn flag.

One cigarette. Two cigarettes if you like.
The mountain. Passing clouds.
Streetlights came on too soon, it was barely dusk.

They're renovating the dairy. Look in: three men at work on the floor.
The tables stand out in the rain. Girls stop
to watch their broken reflections in the wet.

*

Bodies were always moved at night: we had a method for that.
There was a time when Petros
would make victory speeches. He never had any doubt.

Locked away in his room, he would give it all he'd got.
We haven't seen him since then.
We breathe the same stale air. And poetry's a write-off.

Testament

I believe in love, he said, and I believe in death.
I believe in poetry, so I believe in the immortal.

I write lines: I exist. I write the world: the world exists.
A river flows from my fingertip. The sky is impossibly blue.

This vision is all I have and all I need.

CPSIA information can be obtained
at www.ICGtesting.com
Printed in the USA
JSHW022248250723
45367JS00001B/1